Sound Like a Sailor

Sound Like a Sailor

The Book of Nautical Expressions

R. Bruce Macdonald

HARBOUR
PUBLISHING

1 2 3 4 5 — 29 28 27 26 25

HARBOUR PUBLISHING CO. LTD.
P.O. Box 219, Madeira Park, BC, V0N 2H0
www.harbourpublishing.com

Edited by Derek Fairbridge
Cover design by Anna Comfort O'Keeffe
Text design by Libris Simas Ferraz / Onça Publishing
Printed and bound in South Korea

Harbour Publishing acknowledges the support of the Canada Council for the Arts, the Government of Canada, and the Province of British Columbia through the BC Arts Council.

LIBRARY AND ARCHIVES CANADA CATALOGUING IN PUBLICATION
Title: Sound like a sailor : the book of nautical expressions / R. Bruce Macdonald.
Names: Macdonald, R. Bruce, 1962- author.
Identifiers: Canadiana (print) 20250158582 | Canadiana (ebook) 20250165473 | ISBN 9781998526239 (hardcover) | ISBN 9781998526246 (EPUB)
Subjects: LCSH: Sailors—Slang. | LCSH: Sailors—Language. | LCSH: Naval art and science—Slang. | LCSH: English language—Slang.
Classification: LCC PE3727.S3 M33 2025 | DDC 427—dc23

For my daughters Maida and Isabel
Long may your big jibs draw

Table of Contents

G

H

I

J

K

L

M

N

O

P

Q

R

S

T

Introduction

When sailors put to sea they were often away from shore months or even years at a time. Within this closed community or society aboard ship, new words or phrases were adopted, sometimes as a shortcut, sometimes as a hybrid of languages spoken aboard, and sometimes as a form of poetic licence. While visiting foreign and exotic ports, new words were picked up and put into common use. When back ashore, either temporarily on leave or upon retirement—known as "swallowing the anchor"—their language followed them and eventually some terms became part of the common vernacular. This book is an account of many of these terms that we still use today. Wherever possible I have delved into the generally accepted history of their origins.

Words ebb and flow with the tide. Some find new meanings as each generation discovers a salty expression and then pirates it for their own use, giving it a new life. These words hold fast, and while retaining their original spirit, their original meaning is lost like a ship overwhelmed at sea.

This book is also an apology of sorts to the number of people whom I have stopped mid-sentence over the years to offer the aside that a word or term they have employed had its genesis in an old sea term before "hijacking" the conversation to explain its nautical origin.

For the reader, I hope this short etymological survey will secure in your mind that you—whether you know it or not—already sound like a sailor, and that it will also hopefully provide some answers to the age-old question, "Why do we say that?"

A1

The very best. In the mid-1700s Lloyd's Register of Shipping came up with the alphabetic and numeric system to classify the condition of vessels. The ship's hull was given a letter grade and her equipment a number, with A1 being the highest rating.

Aback

To be startled, as in, "I was taken aback by those remarks." The original meaning: when a ship's sails caught the wind on the wrong side (the leeward rather than the windward) and so stopped the vessel's headway.

Abandon Ship

A response to a hopeless situation. An obvious reference to giving up.

Abeam

Something that is beside a person is said to be abeam of them; derives from when something is beside the beam, or the widest part of a vessel.

Aboard

This word and its cousin, "on board," can be used interchangeably ashore to convey agreement with a position or proposal. "Aboard" describes the act of entering a ship. After that, the person is on board.

A Bone in Her Teeth

When someone is proceeding or working with a lot of energy and determination. This originally described a vessel charging along and creating a white bow wave.

Above Board

In everyday usage, this describes something that is in plain sight and legal—fair dealing, no skullduggery. Its original meaning was, simply, out in the open or on the open deck. One explanation suggests its current usage is a reference to vessels such as those used by pirates that hid the majority of their crew belowdecks to fool other captains into believing they didn't pose a threat.

Accost

To approach someone aggressively. Originally from the Latin *accostare*, meaning to come up to the side, as with another vessel or the coast.

A Couple of Shakes

Very quickly. When a sailing vessel is heading too close to the wind and her sails luff—a condition that must be quickly corrected or else the vessel might find herself "in irons," or stopped dead in the water. This expression came ashore as "two shakes of a lamb's tail."

Action Stations

When a task needs to be completed by team members, they are often directed to their "action stations." The term originates from naval parlance to order sailors to their respective posts in preparation for battle.

Admiral

Someone with *admiral* qualities is someone to be respected or "admired." This word is from the Arabic *emir-al-bahr*, which means commander of the seas.

Adrift

When someone is lacking direction in life. Originally meant when a vessel was not under control and at the mercy of the wind and sea.

Aground

When a project or a person has stopped making progress. Nautically, it means when a vessel touches bottom, either intentionally or not.

Ahead

To go forward. That which is in front of the vessel. As opposed to "astern."

Ahold

To grasp firmly. Originally a sixteenth-century nautical term meaning to sail as close to the wind as possible. Immortalized in Shakespeare's *The Tempest*, in which the Boatswain says, "Lay her a-hold, lay her a-hold. Set her two courses off to sea again."

Ahoy

A traditional way to greet a sailor. This word comes from the Dutch greeting *hoi* but was quickly and almost exclusively used by mariners in the sixteenth century. It first appeared in print in the novel *The Adventures of Peregrine Pickle* (1751) by Tobias Smollett. Fun fact: the inventor of the telephone, Alexander Graham Bell, felt that people should answer his invention with this word, but it never caught on.

Albatross Around One's Neck

Carrying the baggage of a past misdeed. This phrase comes from Samuel Taylor Coleridge's poem "The Rime of the Ancient Mariner" (1798), in which a sailor who shot an albatross (which were thought to bring good luck and carried the souls of drowned sailors) is forced by his crew to wear the dead bird around his neck as a reminder of his transgression.

All Arms and Legs

Awkward, gangly adolescents are often described this way, but this old expression originally referred to a vessel carrying too much sail and looking ungainly.

All at Sea

Confused or lost. This phrase dates back to the 1700s and refers to a vessel being out of sight of land and the crew unsure of their position.

All Hands on Deck

When a job needs to be done immediately and all must pitch in. A common nautical order when the whole crew is urgently needed to muster.

All in a Day's Work

This idiom may have come from describing a ship's run, which is recorded from noon to noon and includes all of the sun and lunar sights.

All Sewn Up

When a job is completed. Originally used to describe when a dead sailor was sewn into his hammock prior to being buried at sea. Grisly tidbit: the last stitch was always thrust through the late sailor's nose to ensure that he was in fact deceased.

All Washed Up

Someone who is no longer effective. This was an expression used to describe a shipwrecked sailor who only had the clothes on his back.

Aloof

Describes a person who is emotionally distant or a snob. There are three possible nautical origins to this word: the first being an evolution from a Dutch word, *loef*, which describes a vessel that chose to keep windward of others; another being a contraction of "all off," meaning to stand clear of danger; it was also an order for the helmsman to be watchful of the luff of the sail.

Antenna

This word—which these days more commonly refers to a rod or wire that transmits or receives radio signals (or to the feelers on an insect)—originates from the Latin word *antemna*, which refers to the sail yard or spar that is part of the lateen rig, a triangular sail set.

Any Port in a Storm

When things are going badly and any help is accepted. At sea: to seek help or safe harbour anywhere when in danger.

Armed to the Teeth

Some linguists believe this originates from a description of fourteenth-century knights in full armour, while others trace it only to the 1700s, when Caribbean pirates would augment their one-shot pistols with a plethora of blades, including one carried between the teeth.

Arrive

This word, once only used nautically, comes from the Latin *arripare*, meaning to come ashore.

Arsenal

From the Italian word for wharf, *arzenale*. It is now the word for a storehouse for ammunition, or a collection of skills or resources that someone or a team has at their disposal.

As the Crow Flies

The most direct route. Early sailors would sometimes carry crows aboard and release them to establish the direction toward the closest land, as the bird would fly there in a straight line.

At a Rate of Knots

Very quickly. Describes a ship's velocity measured with a chip log, which was a device trailed astern of a ship. The knots tied at specific intervals on the line attached to it were counted off to determine speed.

At Loggerheads

To be in dispute with. A loggerhead is an iron tool that is heated to melt tar aboard for re-seaming the decks. It could also be a dangerous shipboard weapon, and if two sailors were having a disagreement, the threat of one of these tools being put to use was very real.

At Loose Ends

Today this describes a person who doesn't know what to do with their time. Originally the phrase described lines or ropes that had been left in a disorderly, unseamanlike fashion.

Awash

To be inundated or overwhelmed. Originally from the fifteenth century, this nautical word means "flush with" and was primarily used to describe where the sea met low-lying rocks.

Aweigh

To get going. Originally described when an anchor was broken free from the sea floor.

Awning

An overhang that extends from a building to provide additional coverage. Began as a nautical word recorded by Captain John Smith in the 1600s as a canvas cover for protection from the sun's rays.

Aye Aye

Affirmative. Old English for yes.

B

Backing and Filling

Stalling or being indecisive. Refers to the process of keeping a sailing vessel as stationary as possible by first accepting the wind on the windward side and then doing the converse.

Backwash

The consequences of an event or, in modern slang terms, when fluid is transferred back to a drinking container from the mouth. The word refers to the motion of a receding wave and also the effect of the propeller on the water when a vessel is moving astern.

Bail Out

Today we hear about corporate bail-outs when a company is rescued with funds from elsewhere, but its original meaning was to remove water from the vessel. The word comes from *baille*, the Old French for bucket.

Ballast

Heavy materials, such as stones or metal, placed deep in the hull to stabilize a vessel, particularly when she has no cargo. Now more commonly used to describe structural support for a building or vehicle, or emotional support provided by another person.

Balls to the Wall

When someone or something is proceeding with maximum effort. Originally used to describe two balls connected by a rod or lever in the centrifugal governor of steam engines. As fuel such as wood or coal is added, more steam pressure is produced, which forces the spinning balls to be pulled to the walls, which in turn activates a valve limiting the amount of steam entering the engine. Also, "balls-out" describes a situation in which the maximum amount of steam is being used.

Balls-Up

A botched or mismanaged task—a total mess. This refers to the International Regulations for Preventing Collisions at Sea (COLREGS) and the practice of hoisting between one and three black balls aloft to alert other mariners to the state of one's vessel. One black ball indicates that the vessel is at anchor; two black balls indicates that the vessel is not under command, which means that she is unable to manoeuvre, perhaps due to a steering malfunction; three balls up indicates that the vessel is aground.

Bamboozle

To trick or cheat someone. This word comes from flying different colours or country flags in order to deceive the enemy and is derived from the Scottish *bumbazed*, meaning to bewilder, perplex or stupefy. It was first recorded in 1807 in William Hamilton's *The History of the Life and Adventures, and Heroic Actions, of the Renowned Sir William Wallace*.

Banyan Day

Traditionally this phrase—borrowed from the Hindi *baniyā*, for an Indian mercantile class who were vegan—meant that no meat would be served that day to the crew of a vessel. It has since come to mean essentially the opposite, with a "Banyan Day" being a time of excess and gluttony, including *all* foodstuffs.

Barge In

To rudely enter a situation. Barges are heavy flat-bottomed craft that have no means of propulsion or steering, and so once they are in motion, their momentum can cause concern or be disruptive.

Batten Down the Hatches

To prepare for uncomfortable or tumultuous times. This is a procedure in which pieces of wood called "battens" are driven outside of canvas covers placed around hatches in anticipation of foul weather. The word "batten" comes from the French *baton*, for a small stick of wood.

Beachcomber

An early term for a sailor who is without a ship and homeless.

Beam Ends

To be close to disaster. When a vessel is cranked over onto her side, either deliberately (to work on the hull) or during a storm when overwhelmed by the wind and/or waves.

Bearing

Today it describes a person's position, but it is a navigation term used to describe a direction or position, by degrees, relative to a fixed sighted object.

Bear Up

Keep your spirits up. From the nautical command to steer closer to the wind. Its opposite, "bear down," means to approach from windward. To "bear away" is to steer farther away from the eye of the wind.

Bedlam

Chaos. This word is only nautical by association, as it was the nickname given to Bethlehem Royal Hospital in London, where many sailors found themselves admitted with what would now be called PTSD or with alcohol-related illnesses. The inmates were often so out of control that the public would pay admission to observe the patients wrestling with their demons.

Belay

To make a line fast, such as to a cleat or belaying pin; also used as a word meaning "stop." *Star Trek* fans will be familiar with the captain's order to "belay that," meaning to stop what one is doing. The same order has been in use aboard ships for centuries.

Bell-Bottoms

These trousers with flared pant legs were designed for sailors to be able to kick them off should they fall overboard. Aboard, they were practical garments when swabbing decks, as the hems could easily be rolled up. The design most likely came about since sailors would be issued a length of cloth with a standard width of fifty-four inches. Cut in half, this made for a leg piece of approximately twenty-five inches.

Berserk

Acting crazy. A word that we get from the Vikings that translates from the Old Norse *bersrkr*, meaning to fight dressed in bearskin or without armour.

Berth

A place to sleep. Originally used in the nautical sense to refer to an assigned place to anchor.

Between the Devil and the Deep Blue Sea

A dilemma. The seam that runs the length of a vessel from bow to stern at the deck level is known as "the Devil." In order to caulk or re-caulk it, a sailor would have to work outboard, so would find himself between the ocean and the seam. *See also* "Devil to Pay."

Betwixt Wind and Water

Today it means in a precarious position (or crudely refers to the area between genitals and anus), but this originally described an area of a ship's hull near the waterline that is sometimes submerged and sometimes exposed to air, depending upon the weather and sailing conditions. It also refers to a vulnerable spot for a vessel to be shot at in battle.

Bight

Originating from the Old English *byht*, meaning a curve or bend, it was first used to describe bays or inlets and then later, aboard ship, to describe a loop of rope or line.

Bigwig

An important person. Not exclusively nautical, this expression was used both ashore and at sea to describe the lords who would wear large wigs as both a fashion statement and to show their social standing.

Bilge Water

Nonsense. The oil, seawater and detritus that collects in the bottom or bilge of the boat. "Bilge" comes from "bulge," which describes the shape of the area.

Billow

To fill with air and swell outward or, as a noun, a large mass of something such as smoke, steam or cloud. The original definition is a large crested wave, from the Old Norse *bylgja*.

Binge

Overdoing something over a concentrated period. Originally a nautical term for cleaning out a rum barrel by filling it with water and shaking it around to extract the dregs of goodness.

Biscuit

Comes from the Old French *bescuit*, for something cooked twice in order to preserve it. The earliest recording of this delicacy is from the 1700s and refers to ship's biscuits, also known as "hardtack" (likely from "tackle," meaning supplies, gear), which were a common staple aboard. The supplier of ship's biscuits to the Royal Navy ended up using the same process, and perhaps the same recipe, to make dog biscuits after he fed some leftover hardtack to his dog.

Black Book

When someone is in a black book they are in trouble. The phrase derives from the *Black Book of the Admiralty*, which listed all of the rules of English admiralty law and their punishments. It dates back to the thirteenth century.

Blacklist

A list of people or practices that are deemed unacceptable. The term was first recorded in 1867 by Admiral W.H. Smyth in *The Sailor's Word-Book: An Alphabetical Digest of Nautical Terms*, where he notes that such a list is "the definition of tyranny, now forbidden."

Blazer

This name for a type of suit jacket originated at sea. Captains often used to try and outdo each other in the appearance of their respective ships and crew. In the mid-nineteenth century, the Royal Navy's Captain John Washington of HMS *Blazer* outfitted his crew with short blue jackets and started a new fashion. Another nautical origin theory of the name is attributed to the Lady Margaret Boat Club of St. John's College, Cambridge, who wore crimson coats described as "all ablaze." Yet another theory is that cricket players emblazoned their clubs' names on the front pocket. Related: the buttons that appear on suit jackets to this day also started at sea when it was noted that the young midshipmen, who were nicknamed "snotties," often wiped their noses on their sleeves. Buttons were added to the cuffs of their coats to discourage this habit.

Blood Money

Today this means money paid to a victim's family by their killer for their loss, but originally it was the cash prize given by the British Admiralty for each enemy killed in a sea battle. A related expression is the "butcher's bill," which referred to how many had been killed or wounded aboard one's own ship after a fight at sea.

Blood Is Thicker than Water

American Commodore Josiah Tattnall III issued these words in 1859 in response to his rescuing his country's enemy, the British, during the Second Opium War. But a variation of this phrase was first recorded in 1180 in Heinrich der Glichezare's epic poem *Reinhart Fuchs*, wherein the Middle German phrase translates to "kin-blood is not spoiled by water."

Blooper

Today this is a funny mistake or blunder, but originally it referred to a light air foresail that balloons out in front of a sailboat when set.

Blowhard

A braggart or windbag. Originally a derogatory name for a loud crewmate full of bluster, drawing reference to the sound a loud wind makes. *See also* "Windbag."

Blow Me Down

A phrase meaning "I'm shocked." Originates from the sea shanty "Blow the Man Down," which in turn is possibly an adaptation of the African-American work song "Knock a Man Down." The term refers to harsh treatment aboard ship. "Blow me down" was also the popular catchphrase of the cartoon character Popeye the Sailor Man and the title of the third film of that popular animated series, released in 1933.

Blow Off Steam

Today this term means to have an explosive fit of emotions or to release pent-up energy. Originally, this referred to the action required when a steamboat built up too much pressure in her boiler and there was a risk of the boiler exploding. It could also refer to when the captain had to reduce speed by releasing a valve to lower the pressure.

Blue Monday

There are countless expressions of how people don't like Mondays, since it is the traditional start of the workweek, but Monday was often the day for punishments aboard ship, and "blue" possibly refers to the marks and bruises left by flogging.

Blue Peter

This blue signal flag with a white square in the middle is raised to signify that a ship is readying to depart. It was first used by the Royal Navy in 1777. Each letter of the alphabet and the numbers zero through ten have their own unique design and meaning. This name refers to the predominant colour of the flag with the letter "p" being pronounced "papa." The nickname "Peter" might be a reference to the apostle who walked on water with Jesus. Admiral Sir William Cornwallis of the Royal Navy was affectionately nicknamed "Billy Blue" by his crew since he insisted upon flying the Blue Peter whenever his ship was at anchor to indicate that she was ready to return to sea.

Board

This comes from the Old English *bord*, which meant the side of the ship.

Bolster

To help or support someone or something. Originally this was the name for gear made of sacrificial pieces of wood aboard ship that were set into the rigging to prevent chafing.

Bonanza

A situation that leads to the sudden accumulation of riches. From the Latin for calm seas.

Booby Hatch

A psychiatric ward or hospital. "Hatch" refers to an opening or hold in the deck of a ship, while "booby" is an archaic derogatory word for a person with mental health issues. The word "booby" comes from the clumsy seabird of the same name that was easily fooled and caught. There is some speculation that the actual term came from sailors being punished by being locked below after entering this small hatch.

Boom

Today "boom" can refer to the pole used to hold overhead microphones in filmmaking. This usage comes from the spar or pole that supports the lower edge of a sailboat's fore-and-aft sail or sails. It comes from the Dutch *boom*, meaning a tree or pole.

Boot Camp

Today we call a challenging training course a "boot camp," but the term came out of the Spanish-American War, when sailors being trained ashore wore leggings called *boots*.

Bootleg

To smuggle and/or sell alcohol. Originally from smugglers working during King George III's reign, who would hide illicit cargo in the legs of their large seaboots.

Booty

Today this word has become a slang term for buttocks, but it originally referred to goods that had been taken from another vessel. It comes from the Old English *bote*, which means stolen goods.

Bottle Up

When an enemy's fleet was held from the threat of naval patrols, it was said to be "bottled up," perhaps in reference to the shape of the bay or harbour they were anchored in.

Bottoms Up

Said when encouraging others to drink. If a would-be recruit accepted the King's shilling, payment from a recruiter, he had joined the navy. To this end, sneaky recruiters would slip a shilling into an unsuspecting person's mug of beer and give a toast. Once the beer was drained and the shilling touched the man's lips, he was deemed to have accepted payment and was now part of the navy. It is for this reason that traditional beer steins often have glass bottoms so the drinker can see if there is a shilling at its base.

Break the Ice

To start a conversation in a formal or tense situation. Originally this described when a sturdy ship known as an "icebreaker" breaks the ice on the sea surface to clear a path for another ship to move freely. Dutch theologian Erasmus used the Latin term *scindere glaciem* ("split the ice") in 1528 to describe crewmen of a boat walking ahead on a frozen river to clear the way for their vessel.

Brig

Using this word to refer to a prison originates with the Royal Navy's occasional use of smaller two-masted, square-rigged vessels, known as "brigs," for housing prisoners. Coincidentally, a similar two-masted vessel called a "brigantine," from the Old Italian *brigare*, meaning a skirmisher or pirate (Latin *brigo*, "to fight"), and thus the root word for "brigands," a term referring to a gang of robbers.

Broad in the Beam

Today this might describe a person with wide hips, but originally it described a ship with a wide width (beam).

Brought Up Short

To stop suddenly in one's tracks. This was originally a sea term for stopping a ship abruptly by immediately dropping anchor.

Buccaneer

A pirate. Originates from the French word *boucan*, meaning a frame to dry or cure meat on, and the term was first used to describe Caribbean residents who used them. It later became the name for privateers who traded with the New World in defiance of Spain, 1524–1760. They would make their home ports in the Caribbean. It is also the punchline to the joke of how much a pirate charges for a piece of corn.

Bugle

The name for this instrument comes from a time when French sailors originally blew on ox horns. The word "bugle" comes from the Latin *buculus*, which means wild ox.

Bumpkin

A fool or a simple person—often expressed as "country bumpkin." A bumpkin is the spar that protrudes off the stern of some sailboats to extend their rigging. This comes from the Dutch *boomken*, for small tree. Aboard ship this word is pronounced "boomkin."

Bun Fight (or Bun Worry)

A naval term for a tea party ashore where there would be female company. Dating back to the 1800s, "bun worrier" also refers to an anxious person and was the name of a character played by Jim Ferguson of the Irish Rovers on their self-titled program that ran on CBC Television in the 1970s.

Buoy (One's Spirits—Buoyed Up)

Today we use this term to describe lifting one's mood, but it means when a float is used to hold the anchor rode off the seabed to keep it from chafing.

Busker

Today this almost exclusively refers to a street performer, but it comes from the Spanish *buscar*, meaning to cruise or sail in search of treasure, much like a pirate. The modern busker also seeks profit from the public.

By and Large

Today this means "for the most part." Originally it meant keeping sails working efficiently. "By" refers to sailing the ship as close to the wind as possible, while "large" refers to preventing the sails from luffing. It is a more relaxed way of steering a sailboat.

By Guess and By God

A phrase that popped up in the mid to late nineteenth century, it describes how a navigator's experience was perhaps more relied upon than his instruments. Now it refers to working by instinct.

By the Boards

Today we use this expression to describe something that is no longer done, but it originally referred to anything that was put overboard, whether by accident or not.

Cable

A conduit. This word arose in the 1100s specifically to describe the large hawser or rope, often twenty inches in circumference, that connected the anchor to the ship.

Caboose

Most people know this as a railway term, but a "camboose," of which "caboose" is a variant, was a stove mounted on deck in early sailing ships, where the cooking was done out in the elements.

Cad

A person who is insensitive to others' feelings. Originally used to describe an area of the wardroom where the young officers could be left to partake in juvenile behaviour.

Calm Before the Storm

A moment of tranquility before things go badly. This phrase was recorded as far back as the 1700s and in many variations. It comes from sailors' observations that, before a storm hits, there is often a period of eerie calm.

Canvas

This term for material that was used for centuries to make sails comes from the Latin *cannabis*, meaning made of hemp. Hemp was a key fibre in the construction of canvas.

Caper

To move about in a lively, playful way. The term was originally used to describe Irish fishermen who worked the seas in any weather.

Careen

To move quickly and out of control. Originally this word meant to heel or lean a ship over onto her side in order to work on her bottom. From the Latin *carina*, meaning keel of a ship.

Cargo

From the Spanish word *carga*, meaning goods loaded aboard a ship.

Carried Away

A situation that is out of control. Describes when gear such as sails or spars get ripped from a vessel during rough weather.

Carry On

Keep going. A nautical command to unfurl sails and get underway.

Cartel

An often illegal agreement between two parties to control price, distribution and supply of goods. Originally this was the word for a written agreement between nations at war to exchange prisoners captured in sea battles. The word comes from the Latin *carta*, which describes the letter or document containing the agreement.

Castaway

Isolated on one's own, rejected by others. From the practice of leaving an unwanted crew member ashore on a deserted island.

Casting Around

Searching for answers. This refers to using, or "casting," a leadline to determine the depth of water a vessel is in.

Cast-Offs

Discarded clothes. This comes from when sailors were pressganged, or forced to board, arriving in clothing that would be unsuitable for the rugged life aboard ship. These items were exchanged for hardy clothes from the slop chests, and the old clothes were "cast off" or sent ashore. *See also* "Slop."

Cat-O'Nine-Tails

A wooden-handled whip with nine strands of leather used for whipping sailors who had broken rules. The weapon would leave long thin welts, making its receiver look like he had been scratched by a cat. As the strands became bloodied, they would stick together, causing even more damage to the sailor's back. A merciful bosun taking pity might "comb the cat" by running his fingers through the strands to lessen the punishment.

Catwalk

Today this word is most associated with the fashion industry, referring to the walkway models use to display new lines of clothing. Originally it was the word for a narrow, raised link between cabins, used to avoid the risk of seas breaking aboard the deck. The name refers to how agile (like a cat) its user must be.

Chandlery

A shop that sells marine items for ships and boats. Originally this was an area in a large house where candles were made and stored, but by the eighteenth century it was a store that not only sold candles but also canvas, paint, oil and other items needed aboard ships.

Cheating the Devil

Refers to sailors using euphemisms rather than swear words on board, since to curse was to invite the Devil aboard.

Chewing the Fat

Chatting, having a discussion. The cuts of meat often supplied aboard ship were not always of the best quality, and sailors eating them would spend a long time chewing, looking as though they were in silent conversation.

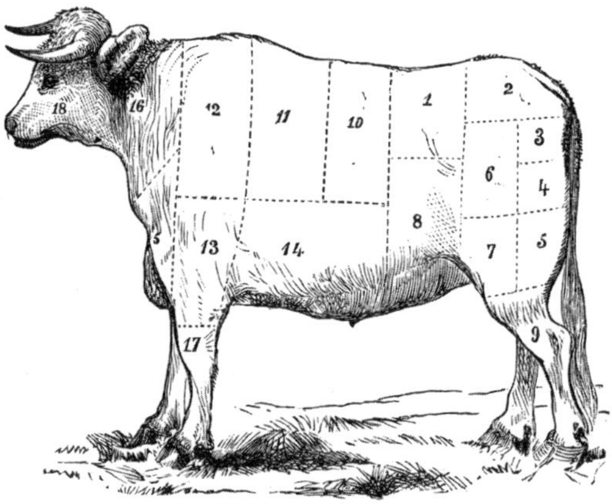

Chit

A short note, usually denoting payment owed. Originally a promissory note from trade with Hindu sailors who would write on thin sheets of paper, and these letters were called *chitthi*.

Chockablock

Describes when two blocks or pulleys are hauled to their maximum so that they touch. It later came to mean full to the brim or having no room to move.

Chock Full

Packed. A "chock" is a wedge driven along the edges of cargo to stabilize it and stop it from shifting.

Chow

This colloquial word for food came from the experience of sailors who were shipwrecked in the British East Indian Company packet ship *Antelope* in 1783 off the island of Ulong in Palau. The islanders shared their food with the sailors—and also shared its name: *chow-chow*.

Clap On

Grab hold of. The order to lay hold of a line or rope and haul on it.

Clean Bill of Health

A doctor's assessment of their patient's complete good health. A requirement in the age of sail was that each sailor have a doctor's certificate so as not to bring disease aboard.

Clean Slate

To start afresh. A slate tablet was used by the navigating officer during his watch, and when his replacement arrived, the slate was wiped clean.

Clean Sweep

A complete victory. This refers to sweeping the enemy from the seas and was traditionally indicated by hoisting a broom to the masthead or to the periscope of a submarine. According to legend, this originated with Dutch Admiral Maarten Tromp's victory over the British in 1652 at the Battle of Dungeness. A broom sent to the masthead is also an old way of advertising that a vessel is for sale.

Clear the Decks

Clear everything away in preparation for an event or task. Originally a nautical order to prepare for battle or foul weather by removing anything superfluous to the tidy running of the ship.

Close Quarters

Uncomfortably crowded. During sea battles, partitions with holes in them were temporarily installed for the crew so guns could be pointed through to defend them when the enemy boarded. These enclosures would become very crowded.

Coast Is Clear

All is safe. A message to outgoing vessels from ashore that the horizon is clear from the enemy or that the vessel is clear of any shoals.

Cock of the Walk

An arrogant person. This began as a complimentary naval phrase in reference to a competition or regatta between a sailor or sailors of different ships in the Royal Navy. The proud winners could strut about with shoulders back, much like a rooster (or later, perhaps, like Mick Jagger). The winning ship would also raise a flag to the highest yardarm with the emblem of a cock on it. It has since become synonymous with being a braggart.

Cockpit

Today this mainly refers to the front compartment of an airplane from which a pilot controls the craft. The word originates with the eighteenth-century Royal Navy and was the name for the operating theatre during battle, because the blood and mayhem therein was akin to the carnage of a cockfight.

Cold Enough to Freeze the Balls Off a Brass Monkey

The fictitious story is that there was a brass frame called a "monkey" aboard Royal Navy ships in which to stow cannonballs in a pyramid shape. During cold weather the metal would contract and the cannonballs would fall out. But in reality, not only is there no record of this piece of equipment on naval ships, but also cannonballs were actually stowed in a horizontal rack called a "shot garland." Modern studies have also shown that brass and iron do not contract significantly in cold temperatures to lead to such movement. Other variations of this term—with different monkey body parts—have been used in common expressions aboard ship since the seventeenth century, but this one is a myth.

Come Up Through the Hawse Pipe

A metaphor for the progression of a ship's officer rising through the ranks of a crew from the lowest rating rather than just stepping aboard in charge and with no practical sea experience. The hawse pipe is a cylindrical passageway in the hull of a ship through which thick ropes (or hawsers) are pulled.

Copper Bottomed

Excellent and reliable. Starting in the mid-1700s Royal Navy ships hulls were clad in copper sheets to protect them from wood-boring parasites and to keep marine growth off. A copper-bottomed ship was superior to those left with only wood, tar and paint.

Cranky

In ill humour. This comes from a Dutch word that describes a vessel in poor trim, and that doesn't sail well either due to ballast or rig problems.

Crew

From the Old French word *accrue*, meaning the members of a ship's company.

Crewcut

A close-cropped hairstyle that originated either in the United States Navy or in the rowing crews at Harvard University.

Cross His Bows

To sail across another boat, ahead of them. When ashore, a junior sailor would never walk across the path of a superior, as it would show disrespect. The expression now means to purposefully provoke or anger someone.

Crossing the Line

To go beyond acceptable or appropriate limits, usually in an act of provocation. In the original nautical terminology, it refers to when a sailor crosses the equator for the first time.

Cuddy

A small space or compartment. Originally the term for a small cabin located close to the ship's bow.

Cut and Run

To flee quickly. This was originally the order that was given to cut the anchor rode quickly and make sail running downwind and to safety when a larger enemy ship is sighted. Described in *The Seaman's Dictionary* by Henry Mainwaring in 1623 as "cut the cable in the hawse; that is most commonly used when we ride in some storm and desire to set sail but cannot stay the weighing of the anchor for fear of driving too much to leeward or the like."

Cut a Man Down

To insult someone. When a sailor in a hammock overslept, the hammock might be cut down with him still in it as a prank or to enforce adherence to the ship's rules.

Cut Me Some Slack

Show me some patience. Originally a request to a fellow crew member to ease up on a line.

Cup of Joe

Often thought to be short for "cup of java," this term for a cup of coffee is derived from the name of one-time US Secretary of the Navy Josephus Daniels, who in 1913 abolished the officers' wine ration aboard and suggested coffee as a replacement.

Cut of His Jib

Sometimes used to describe a person's appearance or fashion sense, but originally this was a nautical term used to identify either a friendly or an enemy vessel by the design of her sails.

D

Davy Jones' Locker

A mythical place beneath the sea where Davy Jones (a pseudonym for the Devil of the Deep) collected drowned sailors and any other goods from sunken ships.

Dead in the Water

Broken down. When a sailing vessel is becalmed or a motor vessel has an engine breakdown.

Dead Marine

An empty bottle of alcohol. As the guest of honour at a dinner on a royal vessel, William IV, "The Sailor King," once asked to have the empty bottles removed from the table and referred to them as "dead marines." According to legend, when a marine took offence, the king said, "Like Marines those bottles have nobly sacrificed and if filled once more would do so nobly again."

Dead Weight

Someone who is deemed useless to an endeavour. Originally this simply meant the weight of a ship before she is loaded with cargo.

Dead Wood

Filler pieces in a ship's hull that don't add any strength but simply fill her out. Much like "dead weight," the term now often refers to a useless person.

Deck

The floor-like covering of a boat. This mid-fifteenth-century word comes from the Middle Dutch *decke*, meaning a covering from side to side over a ship. As ships added more decks and became "double-deckers," this term transferred ashore to describe buses with two levels. We ended up calling a deck of cards just that, likely because of the similar flat surface.

Deck Chair

Broadly, a chair designed for outdoor use, but the term was first used to describe chairs built specifically for ocean liner passengers.

Deep-Six

To destroy or abandon completely. Refers to something that has been lost overboard at a significant depth. On a leadline used for measuring depth, there is no mark for the sixth fathom, so the leadsman estimates the depth and calls out "deep-six" when he feels that the lead has measured approximately thirty-six feet.

Deliver a Broadside

To launch a verbal attack. Originally this meant when a sailing ship of war fired all of her cannons from one side at once.

Derelict

Often used today to describe a rundown building, this word was originally used only to describe an abandoned and rundown vessel.

Derrick

A ship's loading booms, originally invented by a hangman named Thomas Derrick during the reign of Elizabeth I. Derrick had been a sailor and was condemned to death along with some of his fellow crewmembers. When no hangman could be found, Derrick volunteered to hang the others in exchange for his life. He ended up executing over three thousand people during his career and modified his gallows design over the years to use block and tackle, a swinging boom and a topping lift as one would find aboard a sailing vessel.

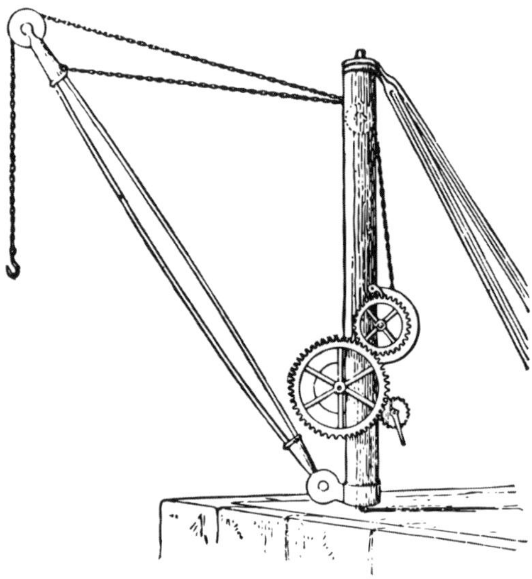

Devil to Pay

The full expression, "the Devil to pay and no pitch hot," refers to the job of recaulking the longest seam in the hull where the ship's planking meets the deck. It now refers to an urgent task or situation that one is not prepared for. *See* "Between the Devil and the Deep Blue Sea."

Dig Deep

To make a considerable effort. From a rowing order to lower one's oars deeper into the water to get more force.

Dire Straits

A precarious situation. "Straits" are narrow passages that connect two larger bodies of water, and "dire" means desperate or dangerous. Fun fact: the rock group Dire Straits chose this name to reflect their precarious financial situation when they started out.

Ditty Bag

Today we might use this term for a cosmetics bag or a shaving kit, but this originally referred to a small canvas bag in which a sailor would keep all of his personal items, such as a sewing kit (which in turn was called his "housewife"). Some sources suggest that the word comes from "ditto," since there were often two of everything needed in the bag, while another theory suggests it comes from the Hindi *dittis*, which was a type of canvas cloth made in Manchester, England, as reported by Admiral Smith in 1867. Another possibility is that it's from the Middle English *dite*, meaning tidy.

Dogsbody

A person who performs menial tasks. In the early nineteenth century this was a slang Royal Navy word for pease pudding—dried peas boiled in a bag. The term was later used to refer to the most junior sailors aboard a vessel.

Doldrums

Boredom and inactivity. Originally the name given to an area around the equator where there is often no wind, so a sailing vessel sits idle. This area is now known as the InterTropical Convergence Zone (ITCZ), where two sets of trade winds meet.

Donkey's Breakfast

Anything made of straw. A luxury for sailors aboard ship was to sleep on an actual mattress. The early ones were stuffed with straw, hence the name.

Don't Give Up the Ship

Captain James Lawrence of the US Navy uttered this famous command during the War of 1812 aboard his ship, USS *Chesapeake*. They were his last words. Shortly thereafter the crew surrendered and gave up the ship to the British. The phrase remains a popular battle cry.

Down the Hatch

Uttered before consuming a drink, usually an alcoholic one. A "hatch" is an opening on deck that allows people or cargo to enter belowdecks.

Dragnet

A systematic search for something or someone. Originally it was simply a fishing net drawn along the seabed.

Dressed to the Nines

Today this means to be well-dressed, but the nautical term refers to when a sailing ship is adorned with signal flags aloft and alow, and some of the crew stand atop the nine primary yards. The term originates in sixteenth-century Scotland, where "to the nines" (for an unknown reason) meant perfection.

Dressing-Down

A harsh verbal reprimand. Originally describes the practice of rejuvenating old sails by treating them with linseed oil and beeswax.

Drunk as a Fiddler

While the crew of a ship manned the capstan, a fiddler would often play them a tune to help them keep time and to buoy their spirits. He would be treated to part of their rum rations for his efforts. This expression first appears in the 1800s and most likely started ashore in pubs or fairs where musicians would play for their libations.

Duffle Bag

Duffel is a city in Flanders, Belgium, that produced the sturdy woolen cloth that seabags and clothing were made from.

Dungarees

An old-fashioned word for jeans. It comes from the Hindi *dungri*, a heavy cotton fabric made in India. Sails were made from this tan material, and the offcuts or the used sails were made into clothes and hammocks by the sailors.

Dunnage

Waste material. Originally referred to loose wood placed atop the ballast so that cargo could be stowed upon it.

Dutch Courage

Confidence gained from drinking alcohol. A derogatory term that implied that Dutch sailors didn't have the courage to fight unless they had been drinking. It was first used by British soldiers fighting in the Anglo-Dutch Wars of the seventeenth century but quickly migrated to the sea.

Dutchman's Breeches

An old sailing expression that describes an overcast sky with patches of blue throughout.

E

Ebb and Flow

Highs and lows of life. A reference to the shifting tides.

Embark

To go aboard a vessel. From the French *embarquer*, with *barque* meaning a ship or vessel.

Enough to Sink a Ship

An excessive amount. At first the idiom was "enough to sink a battleship" but was eventually shortened to this more common modern phrasing. Fun fact: battleships were originally known as "line-of-battle ships." In the First World War, fighter and bomber planes were referred to in newspapers as "battleplanes" but the term did not stick.

Even Keel

All is well, everything is calm. When applied to a person, it describes someone who is low-key, especially in a challenging situation. This term has been used since the 1860s to note stability and refers to a ship being well ballasted so that she does not heel from one side to the other when at rest.

F

Facing a Strong Headwind

Encountering difficulties ahead. A sailing ship steering windward and facing gusts from that direction has hard work ahead of her.

Fairlead

A guide. This is a piece of marine hardware that allows lines to be led so as to reduce chafe.

Fairway

An archaic term for a navigable channel, but now it's most likely better known as a golfing term.

Fairweather Friends

Friends who are only available when things are going well. This phrase was first recorded in the eighteenth century and refers to smooth sailing in nice weather.

Fall Foul

To get into trouble. A nautical term for when one vessel impedes the progress of another, and also for when an anchor rode gets wrapped around the flukes of an anchor. The fouled anchor symbol was first used as the seal of the Lord High Admiral of Scotland in the fifteenth century and became the official seal of Lord Admiral Charles Howard of Effingham one hundred years later. It symbolizes the strong and steadfast character of the navy in challenging conditions such as a fouled anchor or other problems at sea. A fouled anchor—nicknamed the "sailor's disgrace"—is also considered a Christian symbol that recognizes the martyrdom of Pope Clement I, who was killed by being tied to an anchor and cast into the Black Sea in 100 CE.

Fall in With

To meet someone by chance. Originally the expression for when two vessels first sighted one another and, in some cases, joined company.

Fathom

To understand. Originally an Old English word, *fæðm*, meaning embrace, and defined by British Parliament as "the length of a man's arms around the object of his affections," which was noted to be around six feet. It is likewise the average width of a man's arm span.

Feeling Blue

Sad or depressed. When a captain was lost at sea, the ship would fly a blue ensign and, in some cases (such as with a merchant vessel if the owner had died or if the deceased had been born aboard the vessel), display a blue band around the hull.

Feeling Groggy

Hungover. *See* "Grog."

Fend Off

To defend oneself from an attack. Originally this term meant to prevent a vessel from striking another object, such as rocks or a pier, with sacrificial pieces of wood or rolls of canvas. "Fender" is a Galician-Portuguese word from the thirteenth century meaning to split or separate.

Fiddler's Green

The afterlife for sailors, where they can meet former and now-deceased shipmates. According to the English folk song of the same name, it's a place "where the girls are all pretty and the beer it is free."

Figurehead

An elected or appointed leader who has no real power. This word originally referred to the ornamental carving of a person or animal mounted at the bow of a ship to inspire confidence in the crew.

Filibuster

This word is used almost exclusively in a political context—as the name of a delay tactic for preventing a ratified decision—but it comes from the French *flibustier*, which came from a Dutch word, *vrijbuiter*, meaning freebooter or pirate.

First Rate

Today this means high quality, but the term was originally used to categorize Royal Navy ships that held aboard the highest possible number of cannons.

Fish or Cut Bait

To stop hesitating and either take decisive action or abandon an undertaking completely.

Fits the Bill

Suitable for a given situation. Refers to the bills of lading aboard ship that were checked off as cargo was discharged. If all was in order it was said to "fit the bill."

Flake Out

To lie down, usually in exhaustion. The original term refers to a method of laying out the anchor chain or rode in a flat pattern on deck so that it runs out freely when needed.

Flimsy

Light or easily damaged. This was the word for the certificate—a thin sheet of paper—that a sailor took with him from ship to ship that gave a captain's description of the bearer's sea experience as well as his physical description.

Flogging a Dead Horse

Today this means engaging in a useless activity, and the obvious but not entirely accurate explanation of the phrase's genesis would be that whipping a dead animal is not going to make it run. The true origin: A sailor signing aboard would often be given an advance on pay in order to outfit himself for the voyage (usually from the ship's store or slops chest). When this debt—referred to as a horse—was paid off, which often took several months, a celebration would be held to signify that the "horse" was dead. Sometimes a mock horse would be rigged up for the sailor to mime flogging it. There's an old sea shanty with the refrain "I say old man, your horse is dead—and we say so and we says so and we hope so."

Flotsam and Jetsam

Unwanted items. Two specific types of marine debris. "Flotsam," from the word "float," refers to items not deliberately thrown overboard (such as debris from a shipwreck or windstorm), while "jetsam," from the word "jettison," refers to items that have been intentionally put into the sea.

Fluke

This can refer to the arm of an anchor that sticks into the seabed. The term may have come from the fish of the same name. In contemporary usage it most commonly refers to a lucky stroke, perhaps in reference to a whale swimming away quickly from danger using its tail or "fluke."

Fly-by-Night

A shady business that is at risk of leaving town unannounced. This term originally referred to setting a small sail overnight that was easily handled by a small crew.

Flying Colours

Extremely successful. The term originates from when ships returning from a prosperous or victorious voyage, either through discovery or battle, would enter port with their colourful signal flags flying. It also refers to when two ships pass at sea and each displays their respective country's flag.

Flying Dutchman

An ominous tall tale. In the legend of the same name, Captain Hendrik Vander Decken was attempting to round the Cape of Good Hope but was thwarted by the weather. He swore that he would keep sailing until the end of time if that's what it would take. The Devil heard him and made it so.

Foghorn

This piece of gear for use aboard ships and from lighthouses ashore warns vessels of obstacles or possible collisions during low-visibility weather conditions. The steam-powered foghorn was invented by Canadian Robert Foulis. He was inspired one foggy evening as he was walking home when he could hear his daughter playing piano and realised that the lower notes carried farther in the fog. His invention was first installed at Partridge Island, New Brunswick, in 1859 and was soon copied and used in lighthouses and ships worldwide. A "foghorn" is also a colloquial term for a loudmouth. The cartoon character Foghorn Leghorn is an anthropomorphic rooster with a blustering personality. He was modelled after another fictitious character, Senator Claghorn, a bloviating politician.

Footloose (and Fancy Free)

For landlubbers, this idiom means free of responsibility. From a nautical perspective it refers to the foot or lower edge of a sail not being secured to a horizontal spar such as a boom, rendering it not easily drawn taut (and, perhaps, dancing around like Kevin Bacon's legs).

Foul-Up

A mistake. Originally refers to when an anchor cable gets wrapped around the flukes of an anchor, making it unusable.

Founder

To fail, particularly in a business venture. Nautically speaking, this describes when a vessel fills with water and sinks.

Freight

To load a vessel with goods for transport. From an Old English word, *fraught*, meaning to load a ship.

From Stem to Stern

All encompassing, throughout. The stem is the absolute front of a vessel, where she meets the water, and the stern is the very back.

Fudge

To conceal the truth. In the 1660s, British politician and noted diarist Samuel Pepys, then the Clerk of the Acts to the Navy Board, received a report from one Captain Fudge that was so full of lies that Pepys began to use "fudge" as a verb to mean the telling of mistruths.

Full Steam Ahead

Full of vigour and enthusiasm. When a steam vessel is running at maximum power.

Gadget

A mechanical or electronic device. This word was taken from the French *gâche*, which was first used aboard ships to mean hooks.

Gaff

A blunder. This word was used centuries before its modern meaning to refer to a boathook or an upper horizontal spar on a fore-and-aft rigged sail. Aboard fishing vessels a "gaff" is a pole with a hook at one end that is used for bringing fish aboard.

Galoot

An unliked crew or team member. This word was used to describe a person who came aboard with no seamanship skills. Likely from the Spanish *galeoto*, meaning "galley slave."

Garbled

Mixed up. Originally referred to when garbage was mixed in with a ship's cargo to make it seem full or complete.

Gasket

Now most commonly known as a seal for metal joints, this word originated at sea in the 1620s referring to a small rope that is still used today to secure furled sails.

Get Cracking

To get going. When ships had to travel quickly, perhaps to relay a message, they would "crack" on more sail, which is a reference to the sound a sail makes when it first fills with wind.

Get the Lead Out

Hurry up. This refers to getting the leadline out to take soundings to find out if the ship is entering shallow water.

Getting Hitched

Hitching or tying two objects together. A sailor's way of saying getting married. When two lines or ropes are separated into their strands then locked together prior to splicing, they are also said to be "married."

Get the Point

Understand. In nautical terms there is an apocryphal story that in a court martial trial, when the Admirals had returned with their verdict, they would warn the accused of what to expect if he had been found guilty by pointing the tip of a blade toward the accused so that he could brace himself for the bad news.

Gimlet

A cocktail made of gin and lime cordial. Named for the Royal Navy surgeon Rear Admiral Sir Thomas Gimlette, who added lime to the shipboard gin in order to combat scurvy.

Gingerbread Work

Ornamental carvings on houses. This term was first used at sea in 1748 to describe the intricate carvings around a ship's bow and stern.

Give a Wide Berth

To avoid or stay away from someone or something. Originally it referred to either giving enough swinging room for other vessels at anchor or to having enough sea-room from a lee shore or other danger.

Give Quarter

To show mercy. Nautically speaking, to show respect to a vanquished enemy, victorious captors would sometimes grant access to "quarters" aboard ship—a safe place. However, if the order was to "give no quarter," it meant a fight to the death.

Give Some Latitude

To grant someone space. From the Latin *latitudo*, meaning breadth.

Give the Slip

A "slip" is now known as a dock space, but originally it referred to a narrow opening, and to "give the slip" was to escape through this slim gap, perhaps in a smaller vessel, where a larger one could not follow.

Go Belly-Up

To go out of business; to die. This is a reference to how dead fish rise to the surface.

Go by the Board

To fall or be thrown overboard. Today it describes anything that has been lost or discarded.

Godsend

We now know this word to mean unexpected good fortune, but it was originally used in 1812 to refer to goods washed ashore from a shipwreck, a bounty for those who lived along the coast.

Go Great Guns

To move along successfully and with strength. This British naval phrase refers to a large storm in which the thunder resembles cannon fire.

Go with the Flow

To get along and avoid disagreement or conflict. Originally a term to describe sailing with the current rather than against it.

Government

From the Old French *governer*, meaning to steer or be at the helm of (as a vessel).

Grapple

Today this means to struggle to gain control over something or someone. The word is derived from the "grapnel hook" used aboard ship when attaching oneself to an enemy ship during battle or for scouring beneath the water's surface for lost items.

Grease the Ways

To make a project easier. A ship is generally launched from a shipyard via the "ways"—also known as "slipways"—an inclined set of tracks. In order to make the vessel's transition to the water easier, the ways are often greased.

Gripe

A complaint. A sailing term that describes a vessel with weather helm that constantly drives up too close to the wind. From the Old English *gripan*, meaning to grasp.

Grog

Watered-down rum named for Britain's Admiral Edward Vernon, whose nickname was "Old Grog" because he wore a cloak made of a coarse fabric known as "grogram." In 1740 Vernon ordered that full-strength rum was no longer to be issued to his sailors. This is also where the word "groggy" comes from, as well as the term "grog blossom," which was used to describe the purple and red spots that appear on a heavy drinker's nose.

Grommet

A metal eyelet affixed in fabric to prevent wear from rope or cable. From the Portuguese word for a novice seaman, *grumete*.

Groundswell

A spontaneous increase in a particular opinion among the population. From the nautical term describing waves that bounce off the seafloor, creating a large swell in the sea surface.

Gunboat Diplomacy

When a government imposes its will on another nation by putting on a show of military force. This tactic began during a period of imperialism in the late nineteenth century when Western powers such as England and the United States would attempt to intimidate another country into submission by demonstrating their superior power, often by having their naval ships blockade a port.

H

Hail From

To call from a distance. Until the eighteenth century this was almost an exclusively nautical term. When vessels met, they would sometimes draw close and crews would call to—or "hail"—one another, and the question of where they were each from would often be addressed.

Halcyon Days

A happy or idyllic period. In Greek mythology, Alcyone was married to Ceyx, who drowned at sea. In grief, she took her own life by throwing herself into the sea. The gods transformed them into *halcyons*, which was the Greek word for kingfishers. Zeus commanded that during the kingfishers' breeding season the wind would not blow for fourteen days—hence a period of calm. Bonus fact: the star Alcyon was once thought to be the central star in the universe.

Half-Mast

The position of a flag flown halfway down a flagpole as a public expression of mourning. This tradition likely originated in the seventeenth century when sailors lowered flags to beneath the summit of the ship's mast to show sorrow and respect for someone who had died.

Half Seas Over

Intoxicated. In a strictly nautical sense, it refers to being halfway toward one's objective but originally meant being halfway across an ocean.

Hammock

This sling-like sleeping contraption was introduced to Europe by Christopher Columbus, who first saw them being used by the Indigenous population in the West Indies. He recognized how functional these beds would be aboard ship, as sailors could rock back and forth in them in heavy seas rather than being thrown out of their wooden bunks.

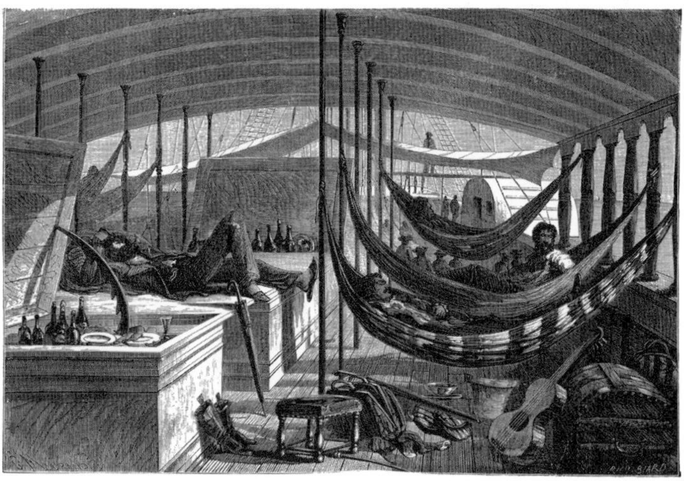

Hand Over Fist

Quickly. Refers to climbing aloft by making a fist around the shrouds with one hand while the other hand reaches up to the next level. A variation of this is "hand over hand."

Handsomely

A nautical term meaning to perform a manoeuvre carefully and slowly. The opposite involves the optimistic expectation that the crew work quickly and with a will.

Happy Hour

Today this refers to a short time of day, generally right after work and right before dinner, when a pub or restaurant offers food and drink specials. The term originates from 1913 with the American Navy, when the crew of USS *Arkansas* held twice-weekly afternoon parties aboard to boost crew morale. The practice soon spread throughout the fleet.

Hard Aground

To be stopped and stuck. When a vessel strikes bottom and cannot move.

Hard and Fast

With the same word origin as "hard aground" (*see above*), this term has come to refer more particularly to a decision or situation that cannot be altered.

Hardtack

See "Biscuit."

Hard to Fathom

Difficult to understand. Originally a term to describe when a leadsman can't find bottom with a leadline to determine the depth.

Hard-Up

In difficulty, destitute. Originally a command to turn the ship quickly to change her heading.

Hasn't Got a Clue

From the word "clew," which is the cringle or grommet in a sail that the sheets or controlling lines for the sail are bent onto. A person without a "clew" cannot sail or make progress. The "clue" spelling first appeared in the mid-fifteenth century.

Hatch

An opening or compartment generally used for storing cargo. Today, most commonly used as part of the automotive term "hatchback." The nautical word refers to an opening on deck covered by a door for its entry. *See also* "Batten Down the Hatches," "Booby Hatch," "Down the Hatch."

Haven

A safe place of rest. This comes from the Norse *höfn*, meaning harbour.

Hazing

An initiation ritual; often humiliating. Now associated with fraternities, this term comes from nautical history, as new crew members were initiated (often cruelly) when the ship crossed points such as the equator.

Head

The bathroom on a boat. The toilet is often called the "head" because on older sailing ships it was at the head of the boat, under the bowsprit. A communal "tow-rag" made of an old rope end was used as toilet paper and left to tow in the water to clean it between uses. *See* "Ahead."

Heavy Weather

A difficult or dangerous situation; stormy weather at sea.

Helm

Today, "taking the helm" refers to leading a company or organization. This comes from the Old English *helma*, which is where the ship is steered.

High and Dry

Left in a difficult situation without support or resources. Originally used to describe a beached vessel when the tide has gone out.

Highliner

A fishing term that refers to how the best fisher was given the most desirable spot from which to cast: high above the others.

Hijack

To rob or take by force. Possibly from "Hi, Jack," a greeting supposedly used by women toward sailors on shore leave in foreign ports. The sailors would then find themselves knocked out and robbed by the women's compatriots.

Hit Rock Bottom

To reach the lowest, most hopeless point in life. An obvious reference to running one's vessel onto rocks—the worst type of seabed to run aground upon.

Hit the Deck

To fall prone, often deliberately. Originally an order for sailors to report on deck for their watch.

Hodgepodge

A random mixture; a jumble. From "hotchpotch," a word to describe divvying up cargo after two vessels collided. Derived from the Old French *hochepot*, a type of stew.

Hoist with His Own Petard

Trouble caused by one's own actions, usually ironically. A "petard"—from the French "*péter*," meaning to break wind—is a small canister of black powder used to prime cannons. If the operator wasn't careful, he could be blown aloft by a wayward spark to his petard. The phrase comes from Shakespeare's *Hamlet*, when the eponymous character says, "For 'tis the sport to have the enginer/Hoist with his own petard; and 't shall go hard."

Holy Joe

A religious zealot. Originated as nineteenth-century nautical slang for the ship's chaplain or for a person who is constantly proselytizing or preaching.

Holy Mackerel

Selling fish or anything else on Sundays was once forbidden, but since mackerel is notorious for spoiling quickly, an exception was made for this product.

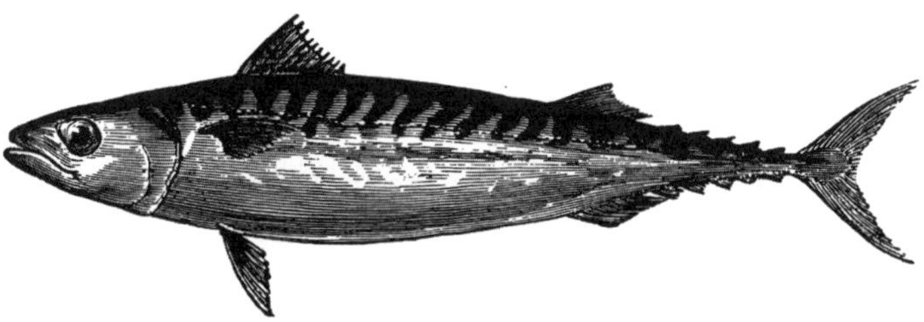

Homeward Bound

Long before Simon and Garfunkel sang a song with this title, Richard Carew used the term in his 1602 book, *The Survey of Cornwall*, to describe his vessel readying to return to their home port.

Hook, Line and Sinker

To believe a tall tale. This is a fishing reference where a fish not only swallows the initial hook but continues to eat the fishing line and weight.

Horse Latitudes

There is a theory that Spanish sailors who had become becalmed in the doldrums between 30 degrees south and north latitude would throw their horses overboard in order to conserve water, hence this name for the region. There is a second theory that by the time a sailing ship had sailed this far, enough time had elapsed that a sailor's "horse," or debt, was paid (*see* "Flogging a Dead Horse").

Hot Pursuit

To follow or chase something closely. A "cold pursuit" described a ship searching for an enemy ship but not having sighted them. "Hot pursuit" meant that the enemy was in sight.

Hotshot

An important person or someone who is particularly skilled at something. The term likely originates with the practice of heating cannonballs until they were red hot in order to set the opponent's wooden hull aflame. These modified weapons were also used by shore batteries to deter enemy vessels from attacking and sometimes placed in buckets to warm the night watch.

Hulk/Hulking

A large or unwieldly person or object. Originally a "hulk" was a vessel deemed no longer seaworthy.

Hunky-Dory

Fine; going well. One theory on the origin of this term: it's derived from "*Honcho-dori*," the name of a street in Japan where sailors had a notoriously good time. Fun fact: David Bowie used this term as the title of his fourth album after hearing the phrase had been used by a local publican with an eccentric vocabulary.

I

Idler

A lazy person. This was the name given to those crew members who worked all day—such as the cook and bosun—and so didn't have to stand night watches. In the Royal Navy these are known as "day men."

In a Flap

Busy, often in a panic. This comes from when orders and messages were sent by semaphore or flags. As the signaller attempted to convey the message in a wind, he would be "in a flap."

In Deep Water

In trouble. Once a vessel leaves coastal waters and is out at sea, the chances of being caught in a dangerous situation are increased, coupled with the reality that the vessel is likely on its own and will have to be self-sufficient in facing these challenges.

In the Offing

About to happen. Refers to the sea offshore, in particular to an object that can barely be seen on the seaward horizon.

In the Same Boat

The genesis of this phrase is often linked to the experience of passengers and crew of the doomed RMS *Titanic*, as all on board faced the same fate, but the metaphorical expression was likely first used by sixteenth-century French poet Guillaume de Salluste du Bartas.

IPA

India Pale Ale. This libation, distinguished by its pronounced bitter flavour, was developed by a London brewer named George Hodgson, who had the contract to ship beer to India beginning in 1780. The British population living in India wanted a lighter beer to suit the hot climate. Hodgson had a small brewery near the British East India Company docks in England and offered them credit to take his beer to market there. In order to preserve the beer for the long voyage he added extra hops to his recipe and named his product October Ale, but it soon became known as Pale Ale made for India.

It's an Ill Wind That Blows No Good

A nautical expression recognizing that each direction of wind will help some and hinder others. The expression first appears in a book of proverbs by John Heywood in 1543, but a variation of it became popularised in 1623 in Shakespeare's *Henry VI*: "Ill blows the wind that profits nobody."

Jack

A common nickname for a sailor. It likely derives from the short blue jacket worn by sailors in the Royal Navy.

Jack Tar

Another nickname for a sailor. (*See also* "Jack.") Sailors would often waterproof their clothing with tar and, since tar was used to protect rigging and seal deck seams, the substance would often be found on their clothes.

Jettison

In modern terms this means to throw something away, generally in the name of expediency, but it was first used in 1848 as a verb meaning to throw items overboard in order to lighten ship. It is closely related to jetsam, meaning the actual objects cast into the sea. *See also* "Flotsam and Jetsam."

Jolly Jumper

Susan Olivia Poole was an Indigenous Canadian inventor who created this bouncy piece of equipment for young children. Though she did so in 1910, the item didn't go into production until 1948. The original "jolly jumper" was a rarely used sail set above a moonraker on square-rigged sailing ships.
See also "Moonraker."

Jolly Roger

This name for the famous skull and crossbones pirate flag most likely derives from the French term *joli rouge*, meaning pretty red. The sobriquet was first recorded in 1724 in *A General History of the Pyrates* by Daniel Defoe, author of *Robinson Crusoe*, originally attributed as "Charles Johnson." The *joli rouge* theory is based on the fact that some pirates would fly a red flag. Other theories suggest that, in the eighteenth century, "Roger" was a common nickname for the Devil.

Jonah

An unlucky person or item aboard. Named for the prophet from the Bible who defied God's direction and was subsequently swallowed by a whale.

Jump Ship

To abandon an organization or commitment to a cause. This idiom from the late nineteenth century originally meant to leave a vessel without permission, often by jumping overboard.

Junk

From the Old English *junke*, meaning old rope ends. It eventually came to refer to any used item that came ashore from a ship. The first junk shops were exclusively nautical; now the word refers more generally to useless stuff. The Chinese sailing rig of the same name comes from the Malay word *jong*, meaning large boat.

Jury-Rigged

Describes something that is temporary or makeshift. Likely from the Middle English *jory*, meaning temporary sail. The term is also often altered as "jerry-rigged," which is based on a slur used against Germans during the Second World War.

Keelhauling

A form of corporal punishment whereby the guilty party was bound hand and foot then dragged underneath the hull of a ship, where his body would be lacerated by the barnacles. The procedure would sometimes result in drowning.

Keel Over

To collapse suddenly. Originally this described when a vessel flipped upside down with her keel pointed skyward. This phrase is often confused with "heel over," meaning to lean to one side, usually from the effects of the wind.

Keep a Sharp Lookout

To be alert and very attentive. This phrase refers to the appointed "lookouts" aboard ship who are tasked with sighting any dangers at sea.

Keep a Weather Eye

Watch out for danger. This term is an actual direction aboard square-rigged sailing ships for the helmsman to watch the weather leeches, or the vertical edge of the square sails closest to windward, to make sure that they don't luff.

Keep Your Shirt On

See "Berserk." Advice to not get carried away in a confrontation.

Knock-Off

To stop working. This was a traditional order to cease work on board. It comes from a time when enslaved crews rowed boats and the coxswain would strike, or "knock," a beat with a piece of wood to force rowers keep their rhythm. A break could be taken when he stopped knocking.

Knock Seven Bells

Eight bells would be rung to end a watch aboard and would also be chimed upon the burial at sea of a dead sailor. To knock seven bells out of someone was to pummel them nearly to death. *See also* "Warming the Bell."

L

Laid Up

Injured or ill. This term was originally used in 1660 to describe vessels that were out of work or awaiting cargo and so sitting idle.

Landfall

The first mark that is seen from sea when approaching land.

Land-Ho

The traditional cry given by the first person aboard to see land after a passage at sea.

Landlubber

Likely of Scandinavian origin, "lubber" is a term for a lazy, clumsy person. When joined with the word "land," it refers to someone who knows nothing about ships or life at sea.

Landmark

This term was once exclusively nautical and described a recognizable feature, either natural or humanmade, that would help the navigator ascertain the ship's position.

Lash-Up

A makeshift construction. Originally this was an order given to sailors to roll up, stow and secure their hammocks.

Launch

To start something new, such as a project or business. This word comes from the Old French *lancier*, meaning to thrust, fling or cast. It is, of course, the act of shifting a vessel from land to water, particularly for the first time, and is also the name given to the largest of a vessel's small craft.

Lazarette

A small storage compartment at the stern of the ship. In Italian, *lazareto* was a word for derelict vessels in which those infected by communicable diseases, such as leprosy, were housed to stop epidemics. Aboard ship, the area was also used for the same purpose and is named for the biblical Lazarus, who was raised from the dead by Jesus.

Leading Light

A person who is prominent or influential. Originally this term referred to a light, often set atop a lighthouse, for showing ships safe passage into harbour.

Learn the Ropes

To be introduced to a new work situation. This was the basic requirement for a new sailor, and when noted on his discharge report it meant that he had learned the very basics.

Leeway

An amount of freedom granted in which to take action. "Leeway" is the sideways movement of a vessel through the water as caused by wind, tide and/or current.

Let Her Rip

This expression was likely first used on steamboats working on rivers in the southern US. When a boat was racing for sport or sought to overtake a business rival, the order would be given for full steam, with the caveat that the steam box might break or rip.

Letting the Cat Out of the Bag

Disclosing a secret that could get the teller punished. Originally referred to removing a whip known as the cat-o'nine-tails from its bag. *See* "Cat-O'Nine-Tails."

Lifeline

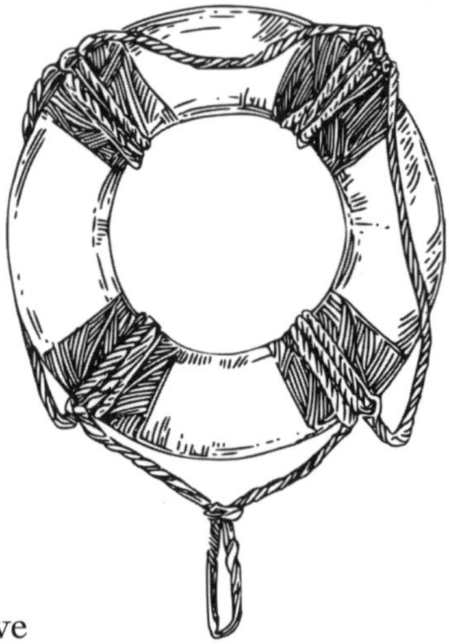

A support that one depends upon. Originally any line thrown overboard to a person drowning or just towed astern in case a sailor fell overboard. The word later applied to horizontal lines rigged above the deck to contain the sailors.

Limey

A nickname for an Englishman, from the British method of giving sailors lime juice to prevent scurvy. Lemons were a better antiscorbutic but were deemed too expensive.

Line

A rope aboard ship (with some exceptions). This term has been used for centuries and comes from the Latin word for linen cord, *linea restis*.

Listless

Without energy. A ship without wind in her sails does not heel or list to one side or the other.

Little Nipper

A child. In raising the anchor, a thin line called the "messenger" was secured to the thick anchor cable with short bits of lines called "nippers" and the knot employed was called a "nip." It was the job of the ship's boys to untie and retie the nippers as the men worked at the capstan weighing the anchor.

Loaded to the Gunnels

Absolutely packed. Originally referred to a ship being fully loaded with cargo. The gunwales (pronounced "gunnels") make up the vertical structure of a ship from the deck up. The "wales" were timbers that ran along the hull of wooden ships for reinforcement. The upper wale was called the "gunwale" because, on battleships, guns would poke over it—this was before gunports. "Loaded to the Gunnels" is also used as a term to denote intoxication.

Log Book

A record of events aboard ship. Vessels would keep track of their speed, distance run and position by documenting this information in a book. Originally the books were two pieces of slate affixed to wooden boards that were attached with hinges. Since the book was made of wood, they were known as logs. A "log" also refers to a chip-log, which was a triangular piece of wood secured to a line and used to determine a ship's speed. *See* "At a Rate of Knots."

Long Haul

Originally referred to cargo ships that would make long passages to deliver their cargo.

Long Shot

An unlikely goal. Early cannons used aboard ship were hard to aim accurately, and it was rare when one fired at a distance would hit its mark.

Loose Cannon

An unpredictable or uncontrollable person. A cannon breaking free from its lashings in rough weather or in a sea battle could cause a lot of damage as it rolled around the deck.

Loose Ends

To be "at loose ends" means to have time on one's hands and nothing to do. This expression arose aboard ship (where there is always something to do) and refers to a task for sailors to inspect the ends of lines or ropes to ensure that the whippings holding the ends in place were still doing their jobs. If they were not, they were to be replaced.

Loose Lips Sink Ships

Beware of unguarded talk. This expression was coined by the United States Office of War Information during the Second World War to warn the general public to not speak freely and carelessly of their personal knowledge about what was occurring in the war.

Lopsided

Unevenly balanced or disproportionate. First used in the early 1700s to describe a ship that was heeling, or leaning to one side, when at rest.

Low Ebb

When someone is in a sad mood or lacking energy. Refers to the lowest tide and perhaps to waters that are not navigable.

Lower the Boom

To scold severely. This means to lower the horizontal spar to which the foot of a sail is bent. The phrase later came to mean a knockout punch, since, if a sailor finds himself under a falling boom, dire consequences ensue. *See* "Boom."

Lurch

This word from the late 1700s means a sudden roll that a ship makes to leeward in a high sea, much like a person caught off balance while walking.

M

Maelstrom

Violent turmoil and confusion. From the Old Dutch word for whirlpool: *malen* (to grind) and *stroom* (stream).

Maiden Voyage

The start of a venture. This expression was first recorded in *The European Magazine* in the 1820s to describe the first time a vessel with a destination leaves port, as opposed to a first voyage undertaken for sea trials prior to a major trip.

Mainstay

A person or thing upon which others depend. Aboard ships, this originally referred to the heaviest and strongest of the stays that secured the mainmast.

Make Headway

To start having success. When a vessel is actually proceeding and making progress through the water.

Make Up Leeway

To recover after experiencing a loss or setback. When a sailing vessel is headed for her destination, she will often drift sideways (known as "leeway") to her course and so will have to make extra effort to obtain her objective.

Make Waves

To stir things up and cause trouble. This originally referred to casting off a ship's mooring lines and heading out to sea.

Manhandle

To treat something or someone roughly with brute strength. Originally recorded as a nautical word meaning to move something by force of men without the use of levers or tackle.

Mark Twain

When taking soundings to determine depth of the ocean, a reading of two fathoms would be reported as "by the mark two," however on riverboats in the southern US it was reported as "mark twain." Novelist Samuel Clemens adopted this regional idiom as his *nom de plume*.

Marooned

Left alone, usually stranded in isolation. Marooning was the practice of leaving a sailor who was no longer wanted aboard on an island by himself—often with a jug of water, a loaf of bread and a gun with one bullet in it. From a sixteenth-century word, "maroon" or "maron," for a fugitive slave.

Mate

A comrade or companion. From the Middle German *gemate*, meaning one whom you share or eat your meat with. "Mate" was first used to refer to sailors eating in close quarters.

Mess

The area where a crew is served food. From the Spanish word *mesa*, which means table. Crew members who share this space are known as "messmates." An old nautical adage: "A messmate before a shipmate, a shipmate before a stranger, a stranger before a dog, and a dog before a soldier."

Mind Your P's and Q's

Be careful with the details, mind your manners. The origin of this phrase is disputed. One theory: In some sailing ports sailors could drink on credit until their wages came in from their ship; the bartender would keep track of how much was consumed by marking "p" for pints and "q" for quarts.

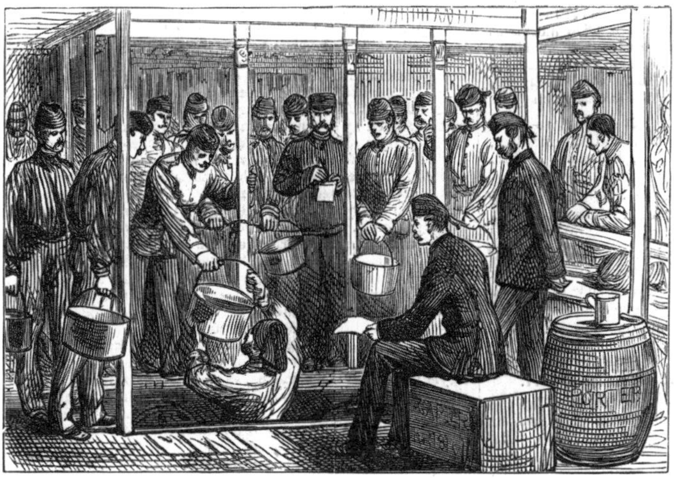

Miss the Boat

To lose out on an opportunity. If a ship was anchored out in the harbour, sailors on shore leave would take smaller boats ashore and then again to return to their vessels. At the end of a night on the town, one wouldn't want to miss the last boat.

Money for Old Rope

Finding value in others' garbage. Old rope or line was sold ashore to be teased apart to make caulking that would then be used to make a ship's hull watertight. The phrase has come to mean that everything has a value to someone.

Monkey Jacket

A short, heavy coat worn aboard that allowed sailors the freedom of movement to climb the rigging. Named for the little jackets in which organ grinders would dress their pet monkeys. In the late 1800s children were often affectionately called "monkeys," and when they dressed up in short coats, their costume was nicknamed a "monkey suit." This term was later applied to the tuxedo in adult fashion.

Moonlighting

Working two jobs and perhaps not declaring the second job's income. There are many theories as to this word's origin, but the nautical one has it coming from the illegal-imports trade, where smugglers on boats would work by the light of the moon overnight and then hold a regular job during the day.

Moonraker

Now best known as the title of a 1979 film in the James Bond franchise, this was originally the name for a light square sail set above the skysail on square-rigged ships.

Muster

To collect or assemble. Originally a nautical term that meant organizing a ship's crew on deck, from the Old French *mostrer*, meaning show or reveal.

N

Nail One's Colours to the Mast

A defiant refusal to surrender. In a sea battle, a ship's captain could admit defeat by lowering his country's ensign or flag. If the flag was shot away during the action, the captain could and sometimes did nail their flag to the mizzenmast to signal to the other ship that they were not surrendering.

Nausea

From the Ancient Greek word *nausea*, meaning seasickness, with *naus* meaning ship.

Nelson's Blood

Rum. When Lord Nelson was killed at the Battle of Trafalgar, his body was placed in a barrel that was then filled with brandy to preserve it until it could be taken ashore. The popular tale is that the barrel was filled with rum and that sailors on the voyage home engaged in a practice called "sucking the monkey," where they inserted a straw-like tube in order to consume the rum.

No Great Shakes

No big deal; of little value or significance. Barrels take up a lot of valuable space aboard, so when they were empty, they would be taken apart and their staves or shakes could be stowed and then later sold ashore, usually for not very much money.

Not Enough Room to Swing a Cat

A description of a tight or cramped space. Originates from when there was not enough room on deck for the cat-o'nine-tails whip to be used to dole out punishment, most likely because of the crew crowding in to watch. *See* "Cat-O'Nine-Tails."

Now You're Talking

An expression of approval. This refers to a common nautical experience when sailors hear the thrum of the well-tuned rig coupled with the sound of the sea along the boat's side—the babbling murmur is heard as though the boat is speaking to them.

Off and On

Intermittently. In nautical terms, sailing off or away from the coast and then back toward it.

Off to a Flying Start

A good beginning. This expression comes from sailboat racing, where the competitors approach the start line with their sails set or flying.

Oil on Troubled Waters

Calming a situation. This is from the ancient practice of pouring oil atop the water to prevent waves from breaking. It was first described in 350 BCE by Aristotle in his *Problemata Physica*.

Oilskins

An early type of wet-weather gear produced when sailors would coat their clothes with a mixture of wax and linseed oil in order to repel water.

Old Hand

A person with a lot of experience. Originally referred to a seasoned sailor.

Old Man

The traditional nickname for a ship's captain.

Old Salt

A seasoned or experienced sailor. The term likely refers to the effects of his extended exposure to saltwater.

On Board

Being a member of a ship's crew. Nowadays this can describe someone who is in agreement with a particular endeavour or course of action.

On the Right Tack/Wrong Tack

This phrase is now more commonly expressed as being on the right or wrong *track*, but in its original form it meant whether one was on a favourable "tack," or point of sail, to meet one's objectives.

On the Rocks

Refers to an undertaking that is experiencing difficulties and is headed toward failure, such as when a vessel runs ashore and all is lost. Drinks served on ice are often referred to as being "on the rocks" since, prior to ice cube trays, a bartender would break off uneven rock-like pieces of ice from a block.

Opportunity

A chance. Comes from the Latin *ob-* (toward) and *portus* (harbour), meaning favourable wind for returning to port. In Roman mythology, Portunus was the god of harbours.

Out of One's Depth/ Over One's Head

Involved in a task or situation beyond one's capability. These terms refer to being submerged in water that is too deep for a novice to swim in.

Overbearing

Overly confident and determined. This word was recorded in the 1500s as "being overwhelmed by wind."

Overboard

Going too far. When something is put over the side of a vessel and into the water.

Overhaul

This word originally meant to loosen lines so that the blocks they were running through were left slack. It now means to take something apart—whether a machine or an organization—in order to fix or modify it.

Overreach

To extend too far. Nautically speaking, this referred to staying on a course too long and so missing the intended port or landmark.

Over the Barrel

In a difficult situation. Sailors were often punished with flogging and would either be tied to the grates or over the barrel of a cannon. The latter was known as "kissing the gunner's daughter." If they were tied to the mast, it was called "kissing the wooden lady."

Overwhelm

To defeat completely. From the Middle English *whelman*, which means to turn a vessel completely over.

P

Part Brass Rags

To end a friendship. Part of shipboard maintenance was to shine the brass aboard, and shipmates would often share the same bag of rags depending upon whose duty it was that day. If there was a dispute between them and they no longer wanted to share their coveted cleaning cloths, then all aboard knew that they had "parted brass rags."

Pass Down the Line

To relay orders throughout a group. A flotilla of ships would pass along orders or messages from one to the other through the use of signal flags. As an adjective, "down-the-line" means complete, as in a down-the-line supporter of a cause.

Pass the Word

To spread information. This phrase came from midshipmen who were stationed amidships, or the centre of the deck, and whose job was to relay orders forward and to pass information aft.

Pay Off

To render payment. There is a negative connotation in the modern context, with the implication that the payment is made for secretive and nefarious reasons. There are two nautical roots to this phrase: the first is to let the bow of the ship ease to leeward when steering; the second refers to when the crew, at voyage's end, would line up to be paid for their service.

Pay Out

To feed out a line.

Peacoat/Pea Jacket

There are several similar theories as to how this sturdy garment got its name. The first is that this sailor's coat was originally made from pilot cloth, which was shortened to "P-cloth." Another theory is that this comes from the Dutch *pijjekker*, meaning coarse wool jacket.

Perks

The bonuses of a job. This comes from the word "perquisites," which in the Royal Navy were the bonuses issued to officers.

Pilot

One who flies a plane. This word was used aboard ships long before it made its way into the sky. It comes from the Greek *pedon*, for steering oar, and described the helmsman and later an expert in local waters who would come out in a small boat to guide a ship safely into harbour.

Pipe Down

Be quiet. Many orders on a vessel were relayed through the use of a bosun's pipe or whistle. In the morning, a "pipe up" ordered the sailors to unhook their hammocks and take them on deck, where they were rolled and stowed for airing and also, in the case of a naval ship, to serve as protection from flying splinters should the ship be fired upon from an enemy vessel. In the evening, the "pipe down" order was given and the hammocks were slung below. Since the pipe down order also meant that the off-watch crew were now allowed to sleep, it became synonymous with being quiet.

Pirate

A person who plunders and robs at sea. This very old word comes from the Greek *peirātes*, literally one who attacks ships.

Pitch In

To help or assist. Ashore this might have been used as a term for working on a farm, but at sea this comes from the regular practice of pouring hot pitch or tar into deck seams in order to keep the ship watertight. It was a huge job requiring many hands.

Plain Sailing

Easy. When conditions are perfect and the vessel practically sails herself.

Plumb the Depths

To examine something carefully. An expression that describes measuring the depth of water using a line with a lead weight on the end of it. (*See* "Sound Something Out.") From the Latin *plumbum*, meaning lead.

Poop Deck

Comes from the Latin *puppis* and then the French *poupe*, with both words meaning stern of a ship. When a wave breaks over the stern onto this deck, it is said that the ship is "pooped."

Posh

Luxurious and elegant. When passengers signed aboard a vessel travelling between England and India, they would try and book a berth on the port side for the voyage there and the starboard for the return trip, as these would provide less uncomfortable exposure to the sun: Port Outbound Starboard Home. While this is a great story, there is no evidence that the expression was ever used to describe travelling this way.

Powder Monkeys

Children. A name given to the ship's boys who carried the gunpowder to the cannons during battle.

Pressgang

A group of navy men who would capture men ashore and "press them into service," sometimes through brutal means. An early form of the military draft.

Press On

To keep working away at something. This comes from the description of sails being "pressed on" by the wind.

Proof

When a ship arrived in port carrying liquor, the customs agent would pour out a small amount and attempt to set fire to it. Anything over fifty percent alcohol by volume would ignite and was then said then to be "up to proof."

Propeller

A spinning apparatus with angled blades for pushing air or water. The first example of this came in 200 BCE when Greek physicist Archimedes invented a hydraulic machine for irrigating crops. Many inventors, including Leonardo da Vinci, worked to refine this, but it was not until 1776, when David Bushnell mounted one to his submarine *Turtle*, that the propeller was used at sea. The propeller was first proposed for aircraft as early as 1843 by English engineer Sir George Cayley, but it was not successfully applied in practice until the Wright brothers' famous flight in 1903.

Pull Your Finger Out

Get busy. This was a term used in the Royal Navy when the person priming the cannon would put gunpowder into the ignition hole and then cover it with his finger.

Push the Boat Out

To order a round of drinks. A reference to commencing a voyage.

Putting a New Slant on Things

Trying a new idea. Sailing vessels heel over as a result of wind strength and the amount of windage and sail area that they have. When a vessel's trim is changed, it is to put a new slant on things.

Putting One's Oar In

Contributing one's skill or advice. This phrase can carry a meaning that is either positive (to assist someone) or negative (to provide unsolicited input).

Put Through the Hoop

To put someone through a challenging and often unnecessary set of tasks. Prior to battle, sailors would roll their hammocks and put them up against the ship's side to protect against flying splinters. To ensure they were rolled tight enough they would be passed through a hoop of a specific size, and if they weren't up to muster, the sailor would be berated or "put through the hoop."

Quarantine

Originally a biblical reference to when Jesus fasted in isolation for forty days (*quaranta* being the Italian for forty). Later, in the fifteenth century, the Italian word *quarantina* referred to the forty days a foreign ship was required to stay at anchor with their crew aboard to ensure they were disease-free. A square yellow signal flag would be hoisted to warn shore officials if the ship had disease aboard, but this same flag is now flown to show that the vessel is contagion-free.

R

Rats from a Sinking Ship

When disloyal people abandon a difficult situation. Rats would often make their homes deep in the bilges of a ship. If she started to sink or take on water, though, they would leave.

Reefer

A marijuana cigarette. This was the nickname given to the young boys aboard, since they were often the ones sent aloft to help with shortening or reefing sail. The marijuana cigarette earned its name from the rolled-up shape of a reefed sail.

Reel Off

Verbally list off. Comes from letting fishing line roll off a spool.

Regatta

This word—from the Italian *rigattare*, meaning to compete—originated in Venice in the 1650s and referred to a race between gondoliers in the city's Grand Canal.

Ride Out the Storm

To wait patiently for a better outcome. It is often safer to stay at sea during a storm than to try and make port.

Ringleader

The person in charge of a specific group. This comes from the practice of "Round Robin" (*see entry*).

Rock the Boat

To cause trouble. To "rock the boat" makes all aboard ill at ease. This idiom is credited to the American statesman, lawyer and politician William Jennings Bryan, who said, "The man who rocks the boat ought to be stoned when he gets back on shore." "Rock the Boat" is also the name of a 1973 song by the Hues Corporation, which became one of the first hits in disco music.

Roger

A word said in acknowledgement of a message received. This was first used by the US military during the Second World War in marine communication to signify the letter "R" for "received."

Rostrum

A public speaker's pulpit or platform. Comes from the Latin word for beak and was the name of the battering ram mounted on a ship's bow.

Round Robin

A type of tournament in which each competitor plays against another in turn. This term originally referred to petitions signed both in mutiny and aboard pirate vessels. Sailors would sign their names in a circle so that, if caught, no one person could be identified as being in charge. The "robin" part comes from when French government officials staging a coup signed their names on a *ruban*, or ribbon, that was sewn at each end to form a circle.

Rub Salt in the Wounds

To make bad things worse. This originates with floggings aboard, where, as an additional punishment, salt or saltwater would be added to the wounds.

Rudderless

Lacking direction or control over one's circumstances. This comes from the horizontal apparatus at the stern of a vessel that controls how the ship is steered and is operated by moving the tiller or ship's wheel. *See also* "Adrift."

Rummage Sale

A yard sale or flea market. Comes from the French *arrumage*, meaning arrangement of cargo, and originally described selling damaged freight.

Run a Tight Ship

When a business is being run strictly and efficiently. A reference to a ship that is well maintained and managed. The old adage "slack lines, slack ship" is the opposite.

Running the Gauntlet

To endure a challenging experience in order to reach a goal. This was another type of shipboard punishment, whereby the crew would line up in two rows facing one another and the guilty person would have to run between the lines while being assaulted.

Run Out of Steam

To lose energy. When a steam-powered vessel can't produce any steam, she can no longer move under her own power.

S

Sailing Close to the Wind

To risk doing or saying something that might get you in trouble. When a boat is sailing "close-hauled," she is being driven as close to the wind as possible, which is a common thing to do. The expression has been adapted by landlubbers to mean that a person is doing something that is dangerous or dishonest.

Sail Under False Colours

To lie or behave deceptively. It was a common *ruse de guerre* to approach an enemy vessel while flying the flag or colours of a different country in order to deceive them. The false flag had to be switched to the correct one prior to firing any shot, though. This technique was employed by navies as well as those sailing under a letter of marque as mercenaries. One famous example occurred during the Napoleonic Wars, in 1801, when Lord Thomas Cochrane, in command of HMS *Speedy*, flew Danish colours to deceive a much larger Spanish ship to let her guard down. Convinced that *Speedy* was a vessel from a neutral country, the Spaniards let her sail on, but a few days later *Speedy* approached the vessel, hauled the Danish ensign down and replaced it with the British one before firing on her, then boarding and capturing her. The practice continued during the world wars with both the US and Royal navies. In the First World War, when Germany was not at war with the United States, the British ship HMS *Baralong* broke the unwritten rule when she flew the US ensign when firing on a German submarine. Both the US and Britain used retired merchant ships to lure German or Japanese submarines to the surface with repurposed vessels made to appear unthreatening.

St. Elmo's Fire

A meteorological effect that occurs when static electricity generated during a storm produces bright orbs of light. The phenomenon is named for St. Erasmus of Formia, the patron saint of Mediterranean sailors. Usually seen in the rigging as a storm is waning, these flashes were interpreted as a good omen among sailors because they foretold the imminent end of bad weather.

Saloon

Most commonly understood as referring to a bar, especially in the Wild West. This derivation of the French word for living room, *salon*, was first applied at sea in the early nineteenth century. As wealthy passengers began to travel by ship, comfortable quarters known as "saloons" were soon constructed for their relaxation.

Salvage

To save from ruin or destruction. This comes from the Old French *salver*, meaning to save. In nautical usage, "salvage" refers to payment owed for saving one's ship.

Schooner

A type of beer glass. This name for a fore-and-aft-rigged vessel with two or more masts is attributed to an American, Andrew Robinson, who upon seeing one in 1713 remarked, "See how she *scoons* along"—*scoon* being a Scottish word for skim—"so a schooner she shall be." A three-quarter-pint glass of beer was originally called a "schooner" in the Australian Navy, where it was thought that a full pint was too much for a young sailor and a half pint not enough. Nautically speaking, a "schooner" is generally larger than a cutter and smaller than a ship-rigged vessel.

Scow

A barge. From the Dutch *schouw*, which means to push out and refers to a small flat-bottomed boat.

Scraping the Bottom of the Barrel

To be reduced to using only the worst options available. Ship's cooks were traditionally given the rights to save and then sell ashore any unused fats or greases from the galley. The barrels that held meat would be scraped dry.

Scuppers Scuppered

To overwhelm, defeat, be knocked out or killed. The "scuppers" are the channels running around the edge of a ship's deck, and someone lying in them (defeated) is said to be "scuppered."

Scuttle

To bring something to an end. This word can be traced back to the late fifteenth century and carries two meanings. The first is a verb meaning to cut a hole in the side of a ship in order to sink her; the second is a noun meaning a square hatchway or hole cut into a ship's deck to allow entry, derived from the Old French *escoutille* (an opening in a garment).

Scuttlebutt

Gossip. Originally this referred to the cask of drinking water on deck where the sailors would congregate and often share their news—the nineteenth-century equivalent of "water cooler talk." A "butt" is a large barrel that holds 108 imperial gallons, and "scuttle" refers to the hole cut into it. *See above* "Scuttle."

Sea Change

A major transformation. Originally this described when a person's character underwent a positive metamorphosis as a result of going to sea. This idiom comes from Shakespeare's *The Tempest*:

Full fathom five thy father lies.
Of his bones are coral made.
Those are pearls that were his eyes.
Nothing of him that doth fade
But doth suffer a sea change
Into something rich and strange.

Sea-Dog

Originally used to refer to a seal, this became a derogatory term for a sailor. This sobriquet transformed into a badge of honour in the sixteenth century when a group of English privateers were dubbed the "Elizabethan Sea-Dogs." Notable members of this informal alliance included Sir Francis Drake and Sir Walter Raleigh.

Sea Lawyer

Not to be confused with an Admiralty lawyer—who specializes in maritime law—a "sea lawyer" is a nineteenth-century term for an argumentative sailor who is forever complaining of ill treatment.

Sea Legs

To "get your sea legs" is to become accustomed to a new situation. English sea captain Woodes Rogers coined this term in 1712 in his book *A Cruising Voyage Around the World*, referring to a person who has become used to the movement of a vessel at sea. Fun fact: Rogers was a well-known sailor but perhaps is best remembered as captain of the ship that rescued Alexander Selkirk, the man who inspired Daniel Defoe to write the novel *Robinson Crusoe*.

Sea Room

To give or seek some personal space. The biggest danger at sea is the land, so sailors try to have enough room so they can always manoeuvre safely.

Shake a Leg

Hurry up. While in port a sailor might have his wife or female companion aboard to spend the night in his hammock. In the morning the sailor would have to arise, but his partner was allowed to stay in bed longer. In order to ensure that a sailor wasn't shirking his duties by pretending to be of the opposite gender, this command was given to all those still lying in.

Shanghai

To force someone into doing something. Life at sea was dangerous, and sailors were often away from home for many years at a stretch. Faraway major ports such as Shanghai were the least popular for this reason. Unscrupulous bar owners would sometimes drug a sailor's drink and then sell him off to a ship needing crew. When the sailor awoke, he would find that he was unwittingly off on a lengthy voyage.

Shellback

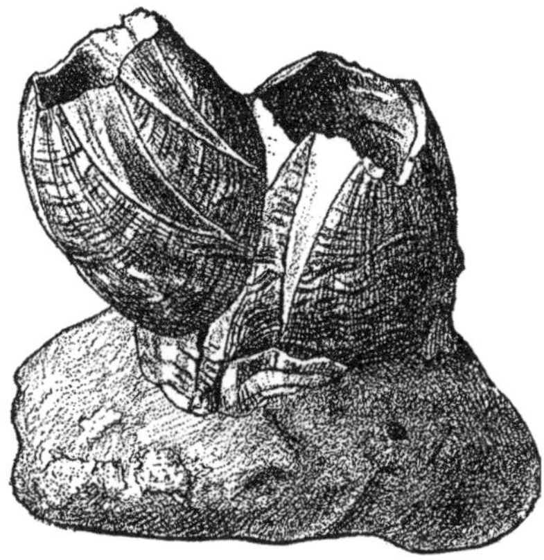

The name given to a sailor who has crossed the equator for the first time. Until this point he was called a "pollywog." The term "shellback" was used to invoke the image of a person so long at sea that they had grown barnacles on their back. *See also* "Crossing the Line" and "Hazing."

Shipshape and Bristol Fashion

Well put together; in good order. This phrase originated in the nineteenth century in reference to Bristol, a seaport in Britain that has the second highest tidal ranges in the world. (The highest are in Canada's Bay of Fundy.) At low tide the vessels would be left high and dry, so everything aboard had to be stowed properly.

Ships That Pass in the Night

Originally this metaphorical phrase referred to a brief encounter most likely never repeated, but it later came to mean an unseen passing. It's from "The Theologian's Tale; Elizabeth" by American poet Henry Wadsworth Longfellow, published in 1863:

Ships that pass in the night, and speak each other
in passing,
Only a signal shown and a distant voice in
the darkness;

Shiver Me Timbers

An expression of surprise (in standard English, "shiver my timbers"). When a wooden-hulled vessel is pounding into waves or strikes shore, her planks can flex and shiver (splinter). This was a common oath aboard ship, but first made it into print in Captain Frederick Marryat's 1831 novel *Jacob Faithful*. To shiver a sail is to let it luff slightly. Tom Waits wrote a song with this title about his contentment with going to sea again.

Shot Across the Bows

A warning. When a naval vessel seeks to stop another vessel from proceeding, it will fire a shot across her bows to warn that the next shots will be into the hull.

Shove Off

In current usage this is a dismissive directive to go away. Originally it was an order given aboard a small ship's boat for the oarsmen to push the vessel away from the ship or a dock.

Show One's True Colours

To be honest about oneself. When a vessel is engaged in a naval battle, she is required to fly her real country's flag or ensign. "True Colors" is a popular song by American singer Cyndi Lauper that describes how she can see the best qualities of her friend. *See also* "Sail Under False Colours."

Sick Bay/Sick Berth

In 1798 John Jervis, First Earl of St. Vincent, Commander-in-Chief of the Mediterranean Fleet, ordered that all British naval vessels have a dedicated space for injured or diseased crew members to recover.

Sink or Swim

This phrase goes back to the 1600s and is practical, and blunt, advice for those learning how to swim as they are being tossed into the water.

Siren

This word for a loud alarm comes from Greek mythology, after the beautiful creatures, half woman, half bird, who would lure sailors to their doom on the rocks by singing to them. In Homer's *Odyssey*, Ulysses had his crew wear earplugs, while he himself was tied to the mast so that he wouldn't be drawn into their trap.

Skipper

The person in charge. This word that originally referred to a ship's captain comes from *schip*, the Dutch word for ship.

Skookum

From Chinook jargon—the pidgin trade language used across the Pacific Northwest—meaning big and strong. This word is now often used, particularly on the West Coast of Canada, to describe vessels that meet this definition. It has been used as the name for three different ferries on Okanagan Lake, in BC.

Skylarking

Fooling around. This term was invented aboard ship to describe the boisterous games, such as "follow the leader," played up in the rigging by the young sailors. It describes the lively and nimble actions of a lark in flight.

Skyscraper

This word for a tall building was originally used to refer to a triangular sail set above the skysail. If it is rigged as a square sail, it is called a "moonsail" or "moonraker," while any sail set above this is called a "stargazer."

Sling One's Hook

To join in. Nautical slang for weighing anchor and leaving.

Slops

Unwanted items, usually clothing. Derives from the Old English *slope*, for a loose-fitting garment. In the sixteenth and seventeenth centuries a ship would carry a "slop chest" to sell "slops," or clothes, to sailors who had either worn theirs out or who had been delivered aboard with only the clothes on their backs. The clothing was often so ill-fitting that the sailors were called "sloppy." The term moved ashore, and even Queen Elizabeth I, in speaking about her court jester's outfit, ordered "sloppe for Jack Greene, our foole."

Slush Fund

Extra money put aside for personal, often illicit use—particularly for political bribery. A ship's cook could sell the galley's accumulated grease and fat, called "slush," ashore, and the money that he made from this was known as his "slush fund."

Smokescreen

Something used to hide or disguise one's activities. This was an early naval tactic by which thick smoke was released in order to obscure a ship so that she could manoeuvre into a better position.

Smooth Sailing

See "Plain Sailing."

Snub

To rebuff or ignore someone. This nautical term means to take a turn with a line around a cleat or belaying pin in order to stop it from moving.

Son of a Gun

A rascal. Women were allowed aboard at the captain's discretion, particularly when the ship was anchored. If a woman needed privacy to give birth, then quite often the most private spot aboard was on a gun deck, hidden behind one of the large cannons. The newborn child would then be given this handle.

Sold Down the River

Betrayed. Refers to a person being tricked and then sold down the Mississippi or Ohio River into slavery.

SOS

This short series of Morse code dots and dashes was accepted as a universal call for help in 1906 by the International Radiotelegraph Convention, but later it became common to refer to it as "save our souls" or "save our ship."

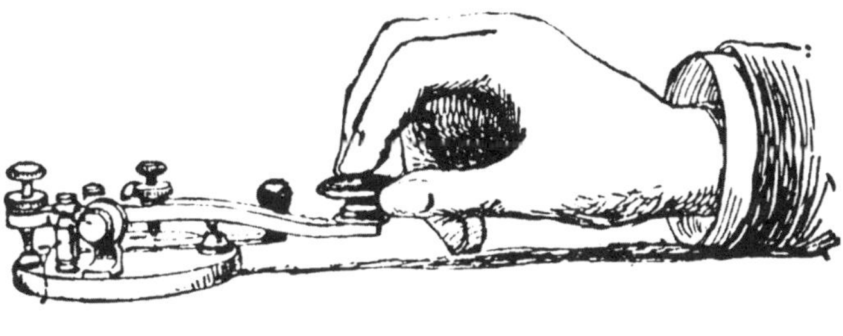

Sound Something Out

To gain more information. This phrase originated with the act of taking soundings with a leadline to determine the depth of water a ship was in and the seabed condition.

Spar

To fight. In the seventeenth century, this word was solely used to describe a wooden pole aboard, such as a boom or a yard (it is also the root word for "spear"), and only much later became associated with fighting. There are some tales that this arose from sailors using light spars to joust with for fun.

Spin a Yarn

To tell a tall tale. One of the many dreary tasks aboard was to break down old rope and then twist it into yarns to be reused. Sailors would pass this time telling each other tales.

Splice the Mainbrace

To serve out an extra tot of rum after the crew has weathered an extreme exertion. When the braces were broken in a storm or they had been shot away by enemy fire, the ship could not be sailed.

Spic and Span

Very clean and neat. Originates in the sixteenth century from the Dutch phrase *spiksplinter nieuw*, a newly built ship, with *spik* meaning spike and *splinter* meaning woodchip.

Squared Away

All settled. This originally described when a sailing ship's yards or horizontal spars were squared or turned at right angles to the deck.

Square Meal

A hearty repast. A watch's meals would be served out on a square or rectangular tray, which was a substantial serving of food. The square design is more easily stowed aboard and a more efficient use of space.

Such trays would also be able to fit into the "fiddles," or raised borders, on the tables.

Standoffish

To be reserved or cold to others. Comes from when a sailing ship was approaching shore but unable to make a safe entry and so would wait by sailing close to and then away from the harbour entrance. *See also* "Aloof."

Stateroom

A large room in a public building for use on formal occasions. In the early 1800s, Mississippi River steamboat captain Henry Miller Shreve named each sleeping quarter on his vessel for a different American state, thus giving birth to the myth he had coined the term. This word was in fact first recorded in 1660 in the diary of British writer and parliamentarian Samuel Pepys, who was an official on the navy board. A "stateroom" was a receiving area or lounge set off from a sleeping cabin and reserved for those of status, such as royalty or politicians. Modern cruise ships now often market large sleeping cabins as "staterooms."

Staunch

To stop or contain. From the Anglo-French *estaunche*, meaning watertight or to stop the flow of water.

Steady as You Go

Keep going as you are. A direction to the helmsman to carry on with the current course.

Steering Wheel

These were first used aboard ships in the early eighteenth century to replace other steering mechanisms, such as the tiller or whipstaff. Eventually this technology and its name moved ashore and into automobiles.

Stem the Tide

To put a stop to a prevailing tendency or trend. Somewhat contrary to that current definition, the original nautical phrase meant to put the ship's bow directly into the current for best efficiency. It is a term that was first recorded in the fourteenth century

Stem to Stern

All encompassing, from the front to the back.

Stick-in-the-Mud

A dull, unadventurous person. This definition was recorded as far back as the eighteenth century. It was also the nickname given to the corpses of pirates hanged at Execution Dock at Wapping, London, on the River Thames. Instead of being cut down after hanging, the dead pirate would be left in place until three tides had washed over his head as a warning to others who might think that the pirate's lifestyle was for them.

Stinkpot

An unpleasant person. Originally used by the Royal Navy in the nineteenth century to describe an incendiary device filled with sulphur, nails, gunpowder and shot and hurled from aloft onto enemy ships to cause mayhem and destruction. These were also known as "stink-balls." "Stinkpot" is also a derogatory nickname given by sailors to motor vessels, due to the exhaust they produce. Sailboats were, in turn, known as "rag-baggers," and steamships were "ashcats."

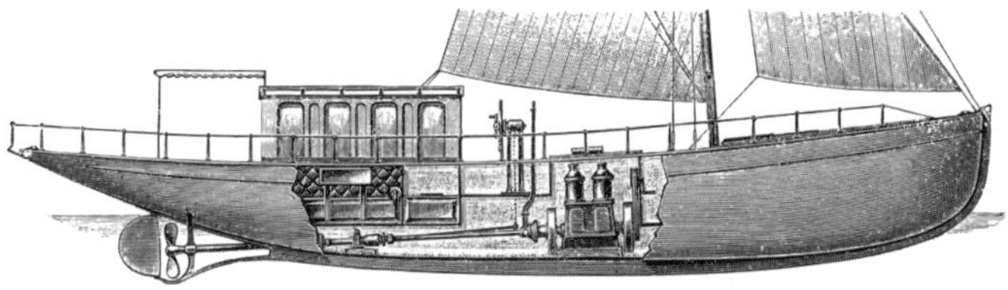

Stranded

To be left without the means to move. Originally to be left on an islet or "strand," which occurred when a captain didn't want to pay a crew member at the end of a voyage or if the crew member was simply causing trouble.

Strike

To collectively stop work in an effort to force better conditions for workers. This word comes from the 1700s, when sailors, in solidarity with their workmates on the docks, would strike—i.e., lower—the sails and yards from their ship so that she could not leave port.

Sundowner

These days many yachtsmen use this term to describe a drink consumed at sunset, but back in the age of sail (well before Gordon Lightfoot penned his famous song), it referred to an officer who insisted that the crew be back aboard from shore leave before sunset.

Sun Over the Yardarm

Time for an alcoholic beverage. The original term was "sun over the foreyard," and it denoted that this was an acceptable time to have one's first alcoholic drink of the day. This was ordered by the Admiralty in an effort to reduce drunkenness aboard ship. The actual order was that "no officer shall partake of liquor until the sun shall have risen well over the foreyard."

Originally the Royal Navy issued a gallon—around four litres—of beer per day per sailor, but by the 1700s it became a half-pint of rum. The yardarm is the very tapered end of the spar called the yard.

Swab

Originally this was the name of the mop that sailors used to scrub the decks, and then by association it became the name for sailors themselves.

Swallow the Anchor

To quit or retire. This is a nautical expression for when a sailor steps ashore for the last time.

Swashbuckler

A daring adventurer or swordsman. A combination of "swash" (the fall of a blow) and "buckler" (a small shield). Originally pejorative, as it described a bully who would roam the streets banging on his shield and looking for a fight.

Sweet Fanny Adams

An exclamation of surprise. Fanny Adams was a five-year-old girl from Hampshire, England. In 1867, she was abducted and killed, and her body was found dismembered in a field. During this time period, tinned mutton was being introduced as a staple aboard ship in the Royal Navy. It was very unpopular, and the sailors, with their macabre sense of humour, named the foodstuffs "Sweet Fanny Adams."

Swinging the Lead

Trying to ascertain one's status. From swinging the leadline to assist in navigation. *See also* "Get the Lead Out."

Tackle

This word that now means to take down physically or to undertake a task was originally used aboard ships to describe the whole of a ship's rigging.

Take Down a Peg or Two

To put someone in their place. Nautically speaking, a senior officer in the Royal Navy would fly his flag aboard, but his flag would be taken down a peg when a more senior officer came aboard and the more senior's flown above it.

Taken Aback

To be shocked or surprised. This refers to a situation where there is a wind shift or an inattentive helmsman, and the sails suddenly have the wind on the wrong side of them, rendering the vessel in a difficult and sometimes dangerous predicament.

Take the Con

To take control of a situation. Originally it meant to take over the navigational duties aboard ship.

Take the Wind Out of Your Sails

To deflate someone's hopes. By sailing too close to and to windward of another sailboat, a vessel can block the leeward vessel's wind, which makes her slow down or even stop in the water.

Taking Turns

Comes from the change of watch, when the hourglass was turned.

Tall Ship

A large traditionally rigged vessel of two or more masts. The term was made famous in 1902 by British poet John Masefield in his poem "Sea-Fever," which included the line, "And all I ask is a tall ship and a star to steer her by," but the term was used generically for any large sailing ship prior to this.

Tarpaulin

A sturdy fabric covering, generally used as a shield against the weather. In modern times this term has been shortened to "tarp." Originally a nautical cloth coated in tar that was placed over hatches to make them watertight. From "tar" and "pall" (heavy cloth covering).

Tattoo

A permanent ink design made into the skin. Sailors had been marking their skin for years, but when Captain Cook visited the South Seas in the 1700s, his crew brought back the Polynesian word for the practice: *tatau*.

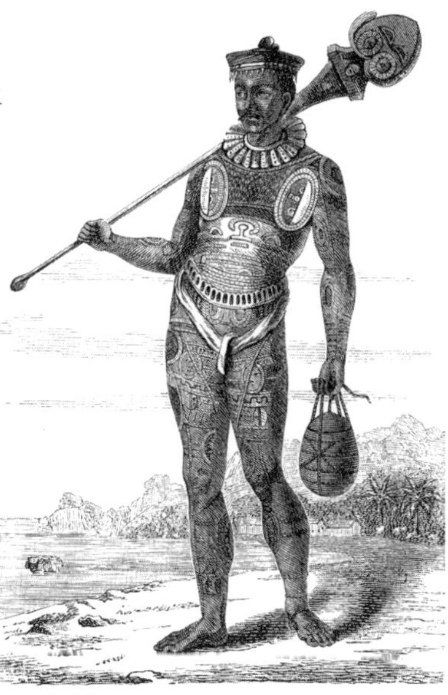

Tell It to the Marines

An expression to convey that one doesn't believe what they are being told. This phrase comes from John Davis's 1804 novel, *The Post-Captain*: "You may tell that to the marines... may I be damned if the sailors will believe it."

Tell Tales

Clues. These are the small wind indicators on sails that show how well the sail is trimmed.

Thar She Blows

There it is. A cry from aboard a whaling ship when prey is sighted—"blows" being a reference to spray from the blowhole of a surfacing whale.

That Ship Has Sailed

This expression relates to a sailor's wife telling merchants that her husband has left but that debts will be settled upon his return. (*See* "When My Ship Comes In.") It later morphed into an expression to refer to a lost opportunity.

Three Sheets to the Wind

Intoxicated. There are numerous, mostly incorrect, explanations as to this term's genesis. A sailing vessel's sails are controlled by lines called "sheets." Having the sheets blowing loosely to leeward means that the sails, and therefore the ship, are not under control.

Tide Over

To help someone get through a difficult stretch, usually with financial support. Originally this term described when a vessel would wait for a favourable tide before weighing anchor.

Time and Tide Wait for No Man

This proverb, meaning people should not delay taking action since time passes quickly, is first attributed to St. Marher in 1225 but was popularized by Geoffrey Chaucer in *The Canterbury Tales* in the late fourteenth century.

To Bear Down

To add additional strength. To approach something from windward, thereby having more control, speed and power.

Toe the Line

To fall in accordance with the rules. Not "*tow* the line," as it is often misunderstood. Describes how the crew of a ship assembles on deck by standing along the deck seams.

Toggle

Today we know this as a short piece of wood or plastic used to fasten a garment or as the process of switching between two modes on a computer, but it began as a nautical word meaning a pin to secure a rope, strap or bolt in place aboard ship.

Ton

Originally spelled *tunne* in Middle English, this word was used to measure how many gallons of wine were carried aboard. One *tunne* was equal to 252 gallons of wine.

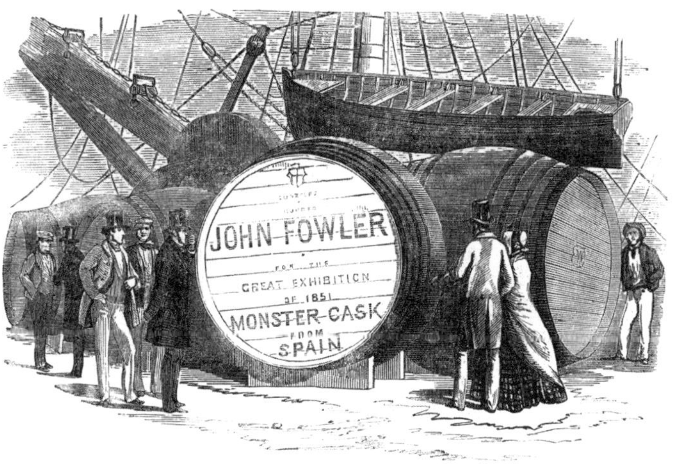

Top-Sider

A style of shoe that was designed to be waterproof and have good traction on slippery decks.

Total Loss

Originally this was exclusively a marine-insurance term meaning that a ship was lost at sea.

To the Bitter End

To see something through to its conclusion, no matter what. The very end of the anchor cable aboard is called the "bitter end," since it is made fast or secured to the "bitts," which are a stronghold on the foredeck. It was sometimes called the "better end," since it sees less service and so is in better condition.

Touch and Go

An uncertain or precarious situation. This expression was originally a nautical one used to describe a vessel making a short stop in port, perhaps to discharge part of her cargo. Other etymologists have suggested that it refers to when a ship temporarily grounds herself and then sails off.

Trick

A length of time. A person's turn of duty at the helm.

Trough

This common word for a long open basin comes from the Old English *trog*, meaning a flat, shallow wooden vessel such as a canoe. It can also refer to the hollow between two waves.

True Blue

Loyal and faithful. Originally used to describe sailors, who wore the blue uniform of the navy and who were reliable and dedicated to their duty aboard.

Try a Different Tack

Try something new; approach a problem from a different angle. Refers to coming about or gybing so that the wind is coming from the opposite side of the vessel. If mariners find themselves making slow headway, then sometimes trying a "different tack" improves their fortune.

Trying Times

A period of difficulty. During harsh weather a ship will reduce her regular sails and fly a small trysail.

Turn a Blind Eye

To pretend to not see or notice something. In 1801 Admiral Nelson was preparing to take his fleet into the Battle of Copenhagen. His superiors ashore sent up a signal for him to not carry on. He deliberately lifted his telescope to his blind eye to face the signal so he could not see it. He carried on—and won.

Turn the Corner

To get past difficulty and start improving. Comes from sailing ships leaving the Southern Ocean and turning at either the Cape of Good Hope, at the tip of Africa, or Cape Horn, at the tip of South America.

Turn Turtle

To be upside down, often helplessly so. Originally used as a nautical term for when a boat is overturned.

U

Underfoot

Constantly in the way. When an anchor is directly under a vessel's forefoot or bow.

Under the Weather

Feeling ill or unwell. When the crew are assigned to be on the weather side of a vessel bearing the brunt of rain, wind and waves.

Underway

Moving; an undertaking begun. From the nautical term meaning not tethered to the seabed with an anchor or to a dock with mooring lines. Fun fact: a vessel is "under weigh" as she weighs her anchor, but once she breaks free from the seabed, the vessel is "underway." However, if she is not moving, then she is not making way, with neither headway, sternway nor leeway.

Under Your Own Steam

Without assistance from others. This term originates from the early steamboat days, when breakdowns in the steam boilers were common and vessels often needed help to get moving.

Unfurl

A word from the 1600s for casting loose the gaskets that hold a sail in place.

Union Jack

This nickname for the British ensign was possibly coined by Queen Anne in the early 1700s. A "jack" is the nickname for a flag on the bow of a ship, and "union" refers to the political merger of the kingdoms of England and Scotland.

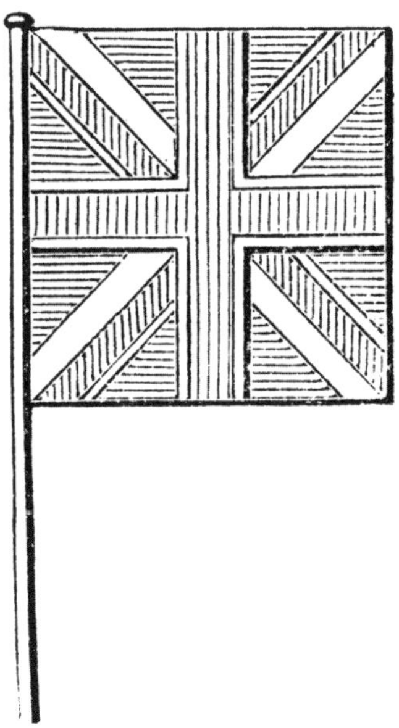

Up the Creek (Without a Paddle)

To be in a difficult situation. This nineteenth-century American phrase was later embellished with the paddle reference and intensified with a colourful name to describe the creek. Much later, and incorrectly, it was attributed to a Royal Naval hospital situated on a creek in the town of Gosport, in Hampshire, England. The actual origin of the phrase is murky.

V

Veer

To change course suddenly. This word has been used aboard since at least 1610 to describe a vessel turning away from the wind. It comes from the French *virer*, to turn. It can also mean to let out or pay out, such as when releasing more anchor chain or a sail's sheets.

W

Waister

An incompetent or useless person; one not pulling their weight. Comes from a person who is of little use to the ship's company, perhaps due to their age or lack of abilities. They were given menial jobs to do in the "waist" or centre of the ship.

Walking the Plank

To accept one's fate. This capital punishment is often attributed to pirates, but there are no records that show they ever actually employed this death sentence. There is a fictious account included in Daniel Defoe's *A General History of the Pyrates*, published in 1724, and the form of execution has since been made famous by numerous Hollywood films.

Wallop

To hit hard. In 1514, during the Anglo-French War, the French laid waste to the coastal town of Brighton. King Henry VIII responded by sending Admiral Sir John Wallop and his fleet to deliver a devastating assault on the French coast.

Warming the Bell

At the end of each watch, the ship's bell is rung eight times to announce the change of crews. In the days when time was kept with a sandglass, a seaman wanting to end his shift early might wrap his hand around the sandglass to warm it, which would make the sand run through faster. As a result, the bell would be rung sooner. It was also sometimes known as "flogging the glass."

Weather a Storm

To survive a challenging or uncomfortable situation. To survive bad weather at sea.

Weather Eye

To be on your guard. Nautically speaking, to be quick to observe changes in the weather by always looking to the windward side.

Weather Gauge

When a vessel positions herself to windward of another so that she is in a better position to fight or flee. Ashore it has come to mean to have an advantage over another.

When My Ship Comes In

A phrase dating back to the 1500s, when companies sought financing for their voyage and promised to pay their debts when their ship, with its cargo, returned. This phrase was used because often no accurate return date could be given.

Which Way the Wind Blows

Most major decisions aboard a sailing ship are affected or determined by the wind direction. In general usage this term refers to the acknowledgement that a situation is out of our hands but that we must make the best use of what we are given and what information we have.

Whistle Up the Wind

A useless attempt to change one's circumstances. This comes from a common shipboard superstition that when a person whistles aboard, Thor, the Norse god of thunder, would reply by whistling back—often with gale strength. The only person allowed to whistle, therefore, was the youngest aboard, since Thor would not be threatened by them.

Windbag

In Homer's *Odyssey* he writes of a leather bag that holds all the winds of the world. This later became a pejorative term to describe someone who talks too much yet says little of value.

Windfall

Unexpected good fortune, usually financial. Commonly thought to have originated from free fruit that had been blown off of tree branches, this term first came into use as a way of describing a sudden and fortuitous gust of wind that came from ashore, usually from the side of a hill or a mountain that allowed a ship to escape a dangerous shore.

Wreck

A word dating back to the 1400s to describe a vessel destroyed or sunk at sea. From the Old Norse *wrek*, meaning flotsam.

Y

Your Number Is Up

You are about to receive bad news or meet your fate. This comes from when the captains of a flotilla were each assigned a number. If the Admiral wanted to speak to you in person, he would have your number sent aloft, and you then had to be rowed out to his ship to accept your fate or reprimand.

You Scratch My Back and I'll Scratch Yours

If you do me favour, I will respond in kind (a *quid pro quo*). This phrase was popular in the Royal Navy in the 1600s. In shipboard discipline, the idea was that "if you go easy with the cat-o'nine-tails on my back, then I will also go easy on you if one day our positions are reversed." This is a somewhat dubious origin, though, since discipline was meted out by the bosun and not by individual crewmembers.

Acknowledgements

For a work like this I would be remiss in not acknowledging all of the shipmates that I have known who educated me in the rich etymology and proper use of nautical terms over our many miles at sea together.

Thanks also to the Canada Council for the Arts for their ongoing support.

Much appreciation to Derek Fairbridge for his copyediting prowess and suggestions.

A heartfelt thanks to Lori Dewar for her encouragement during this project.

Bibliography

Barrett, Cynthia. *Three Sheets to the Wind*. Lanham: Rowman and Littlefield, 2018.

Beavis, Bill and Richard G. McCloskey. *Salty Dog Talk*. Dobbs Ferry: Sheridan House, 1983.

Davis, John. *The Post-Captain*. London: Thomas Tegg, 1808.

Defoe, Daniel. *A General History of the Pyrates*. London: T. Warner, 1724.

Du Bartus, Guillame de Saluste. *The Works of Guillame de Saluste*. Chapel Hill: University of North Carolina Press, 2008.

Gilje, Paul A. *To Swear Like a Sailor: Maritime Culture in America 1750–1850*. Cambridge: Cambridge University Press, 2016.

Granville, Wilfred. *A Dictionary of Sailors' Slang*. Tonbridge: Tonbridge Printers, 1962.

Grimm, Jacob. *Reinhart Fuchs*. Berlin: Reimer, 1834.

Hamilton, William. *The History of Sir William Wallace*. New York: W.W. Crawford, 1820.

Heywood, John. *The Proverbs of John Heywood*. London: G. Bell and Sons, 1874.

Hockin, J.P. *An Account of the Pelew Islands*. London: W. Bulmer and Co., 1803.

Huff, Roger Paul. *Captain Bucko's Nauti-words Handbook*. New York: iUniverse Inc., 2004.

Isil, Olivia J. *When a Loose Cannon Flogs a Dead Horse There's Hell to Pay*. Camden: International Marine, 1996.

King, Dean. *A Sea of Words*. New York: Henry Holt and Company, 1995.

Mainwaring, Henry. *The Seaman's Dictionary*. London: John Bellamy, 1644.

Marryat, Frederick. *Jacob Faithful*. New York: Croscup and Company, 1896.

Nelson, Mark. *Jackspeak of the Royal Canadian Navy*. Toronto: Dundurn, 2018.

Robson, Martin. *Not Enough Room to Swing a Cat*. Annapolis: Naval Institute Press, 2008.

Rogers, Woodes. *A Cruising Voyage Around the World*. London: Cassell and Company, 1712.

Rottman, Gordon L. *SNAFU: Sailor, Airman, and Soldier Slang of World War II*. Oxford: Osprey Publishing, 2013.

Smyth, William Henry. *The Sailor's Word Book*. London: Blackie & Son, 1867.

Telfer, Geordie. *How to Speak Pirate*. Tukwila: Arctic Raven, 2008.

Tierney, Grace. *Words the Sea Gave Us*. Dublin: Wordfoolery Press, 2020.

Windas, Cedric W. *Traditions of the Navy*. Ottawa: Algrove Publishing, 2001.

About the Author

R. Bruce Macdonald is a writer, sailor and artist with a passion for Canadian history. Macdonald has logged over 100,000 nautical miles and, for many years, lived along the BC coast aboard *North Star* with his family. He is the author of *North Star of Herschel Island* (Friesen Press, 2012), *Sisters of the Ice* (Lost Moose Books, 2021) and *Never Say P*g* (Harbour Publishing, 2022).